MILLION
AFFORMATION

THE MAGIC FORMULA
THAT WILL MAKE YOU RICH

DR. NOAH ST. JOHN

with HONORÉE CORDER

MILLIONAIRE
AFFORMATIONS®

THE MAGIC FORMULA
THAT WILL MAKE YOU RICH

NOAH ST. JOHN, Ph.D.

The Father of AFFORMATIONS®

Host of 7-Figure Life Academy and

The 12-Week Breakthrough

with HONORÉE CORDER

Any mention of earnings or income should not be construed as representative of fixed or standard earnings. This book is not intended to provide personalized legal, accounting, financial, or investment advice. Readers are encouraged to seek the counsel of competent professionals with regard to such matters. The Author and Publisher specifically disclaim any liability, loss, or risk that is incurred as a consequence, directly or indirectly, of the use and application of any of the contents of this work.

Afformations®, iAfform® Audios, Making Success Automatic®, Permission to Succeed®, and Power Habits® are registered trademarks of Noah St. John and Success Clinic International, LLC.

To book Noah St. John to speak at your event, visit BookNoah.com.

Millionaire AFFORMATIONS® Copyright © 2022 by Noah St. John. All rights reserved. Printed in the United States of America. No part of this book may be reproduced by any mechanical, photographic, or electronic process, or in the form of a phonographic recording; nor may it be stored in a retrieval system, transmitted, or otherwise be copied for public or private use—other than for "fair use" as brief quotations embodied in articles and reviews—without prior written permission of the publisher.

The author of this book does not dispense medical advice or prescribe the use of any technique as a form of treatment for physical, emotional, or medical problems without the advice of a physician, either directly or indirectly. The intent of the author is to offer information of a general nature to help you in your quest for emotional and spiritual well-being. In the event you use any of the information in this book for yourself, which is your constitutional right, the author and the publisher assume no responsibility for your actions.

Library of Congress _____

St. John, Noah

Millionaire Afformations®: The magic formula that will make you rich/ by Noah St. John with Honorée Corder.

Cover & Interior Design: Dino Marino
Paperback ISBN: 978-0-9715629-1-2
Digital ISBN: 978-0-9715629-2-9

PRAISE FOR NOAH ST. JOHN

"To say that Noah St. John changed our lives is the understatement of the century. Before hiring Noah as my personal coach, I had a brochure website that wasn't bringing in any money. Today, I have my own online store that makes me money in my sleep. Thank you, Noah, for bringing out the greatness in me that I didn't even know I had!"

— Dr. Stacey Cooper, Chiropractor

"Before I heard Noah speak, I had been a failure at everything I touched. After using his methods, I built the largest infill development company in Nashville with over $40 million in sales. Thank you, Noah; keep doing what you're doing because a lot of people need you!"

— Britnie Turner Keane, CEO of Aerial Development Group

"I highly recommend Dr. Noah St. John as a keynote speaker because he's not only different from other speakers, he also truly cares about his clients and resonates on a deep emotional level with his audience. He's dynamic, impactful, inspiring, motivating, and professional—in short, the PERFECT speaker!"

— Lauren Ashley Kay, Meeting Planner

"Dr. Noah St. John has been a Legend in the industry of speaking and motivating for many years. His reputation as a home run speaker, powerful coach, and performance expert is among the best in the world. More importantly, his home life, family, and ability to balance both business and the living of a wonderful life are inspiring to his peers and clients. He is an example to all who know him."

— Jason Hewlett, CSP, CPAE, *The Promise to the One*

"Noah's methods helped me get through a particularly challenging time in my life. If you're thinking about hiring Noah as a coach, trainer, or speaker, don't think about it another minute—just DO it, because his strategies have the power to change lives!"

— Mari Smith, Premier Facebook Marketing Expert
& Social Media Thought Leader

"Noah's methods can transform your life and help you create the masterpiece you truly want and are capable of achieving."

— John Assaraf, The Secret

"Noah's training was instrumental in helping me bounce back and into major profits. His insights on removing head trash are unlike anything I've ever seen!"

— Ray Higdon, Time Money Freedom

"Noah St. John helped me gain the mental edge I was looking for. His methods helped me perform at my highest level without strain, and I saw better results immediately using his system."

— Andre Branch, NFL Football Player

"Before being coached by Noah, I was holding myself back out of fear. Since working with Noah, I've built a multi-million dollar company in less than two years. I highly recommend coaching with Noah, because I guarantee it will change your life, like it changed mine!"

— Tim Taylor, Real Estate Professional

This book is dedicated to #Afformers and #AfformationWarriors
around the world:

Those brave souls who ask better questions

to make this a better world

for all of God's creatures.

And to my beautiful wife, Babette,

for being the best example of a Loving Mirror

I've ever met.

TABLE OF CONTENTS

SECTION II

SECTION III

Discover how my "Core 4 Formula" will skyrocket your results using my Afformations Method . . . in less than five minutes a day!

Use this fourteen-day process (including the single most effective strategy for sustaining your new habits) so that you continue to benefit from using Afformations long after you've read this book

A SPECIAL INVITATION FROM NOAH

Since 2007, readers and practitioners of my Afformations® Method—we call ourselves *Afformers*—have been on an extraordinary journey. Consisting of more than a million like-minded individuals from around the world, Afformers wake up every day and dedicate time to fulfilling the unlimited potential that is within each one of us, while contributing to the collective Afformations Mission—to *elevate the consciousness of Earth, one question at a time.*

As the Father of Afformations, I felt that it was my duty and responsibility to create a channel where Afformers can come together to connect, discover best practices, and support one another.

That's why I created my YouTube channel, WatchNoahTV.com. For years, I envisioned a channel that would encourage and inspire the planet's most positive, engaged, and supportive individuals—and that's just what it has become.

SUBSCRIBE TO WATCHNOAHTV.COM

I'm constantly astounded by the caliber and the character of our member community, which includes people from around the globe and is growing daily. That's why I encourage you to subscribe to our channel at www.WatchNoahTV.com.

In addition, you can hear from Afformers who contributed their success stories to this book (you'll find them in Section II) on our YouTube channel.

My team and I from SuccessClinic.com are always there moderating the discussion, so I look forward to seeing you there!

NOAH'S NOTE

"The habit of reading is the only enjoyment in which there is no alloy; it lasts when all other pleasures fade."

— ANTHONY TROLLOPE

Welcome to **Millionaire Afformations**! What began as my discovery in The Shower That Changed Everything, became a book (*The Book of AFFORMATIONS®*, published by Hay House) and then an online course and coaching program has become a **global revolution**—consisting of more than a million people worldwide who embark on a daily collective mission to *raise the consciousness of Earth, one question at a time.*

Though we may not have met yet, I'll bet we have at least one thing in common: *We want to improve ourselves and our lives.* That's because, as human beings, we were each born with the natural desire to continually grow, improve, and progress. In fact, the word progress comes from the Latin *pro gradi*, "to step forward."

Toward that end, The Afformations Method you'll discover in this book will empower you to step forward to your goals faster, easier, and with far less effort and stress than ever before.

As I've shared in my other books like *Get Rid of Your Head Trash About Money, Power Habits®* and *The Book of Afformations®*, I discovered The Afformations Method one morning in April 1997 in what I call *The Shower That Changed Everything*. In this book, you're going to discover how to use my Afformations Method to achieve goals that you've been chasing for years—and even goals that you may have put away because they seemed too big.

THE AFFORMATIONS METHOD WILL EMPOWER YOU TO REACH YOUR GOALS MUCH FASTER AND EASIER.

Whether you are currently experiencing extraordinary levels of success, happiness, and fulfillment; enduring the most difficult time of your life;

or somewhere in between, I can say with absolute certainty that my Afformations Method is the most practical, results-oriented, and effective method I have ever encountered for improving any—or quite literally every—area of your life and doing so faster than you may believe possible.

Afformations can be an absolute game-changer for you, empowering you to reach that indescribable *next level* and take your personal and professional levels of success far beyond what you've achieved up until now.

This can mean making important improvements in your **health**, **happiness**, **relationships**, **finances**, **spirituality**, or any other areas that are at the top of your list.

In other words, this book isn't just about becoming rich; it's about becoming a better *you*. By waking up each day and doing four simple things that I call **The Core 4 Formula**, you will reap rewards beyond what you may think possible.

> **THIS BOOK ISN'T JUST ABOUT BECOMING RICH; IT'S ABOUT BECOMING A BETTER YOU.**

Whether you want to improve just a few key areas or are ready for a major life transformation—so your current circumstances will soon become only a memory of what was—you've picked up the right book. In fact, you're about to begin a miraculous journey using a simple step-by-step process that's guaranteed to transform any area of your life . . . *in less than five minutes a day*.

Yes, these are big promises. Yet my Afformations Method has already empowered more than a million people around the world to make profound changes in their lives—even when they were skeptical, too.

That means using my Afformations Method can be *the one thing* that enables you to create the most extraordinary life you can imagine. I have done everything in my power to ensure that this book will truly be a life-changing investment of your time, energy, and attention.

Our miraculous journey together is about to begin, so remember:

I believe in you.

Your Coach,

Noah St. John, PhD

SECTION I

THE **AFFORMATIONS**® METHOD FOR BECOMING A MILLIONAIRE

- 1 -

WHY YOUR
WORDS MATTER
(MORE THAN YOU THINK)

"A prudent question is one-half of wisdom."

— FRANCIS BACON

What you think, how you think, and the words you say to yourself and others shape every moment of every day of your life. To say that your words are powerful is like saying that breathing is a helpful thing to do to stay alive.

When you begin to understand the awesome power of your words, you'll become more focused, more disciplined, and less distracted. In fact, you're virtually guaranteed to not just reach your goals but crush them!

IF YOU'RE FEELING OVERWHELMED, START HERE.

For example, do you ever describe yourself as feeling *overwhelmed*? I'd be willing to bet that millions of people are doing that right now. However, do you know where the word *overwhelm* comes from and what it really means?

According to Merriam-Webster.com:

> You could say that the introduction of "overwhelm" to the English language was a bit redundant. The word, which originally meant "to overturn or upset," was formed in Middle English by combining the prefix over- with the verb "whelmen," which also meant "to overturn." "Whelmen" has survived in English as "whelm," a verb which is largely synonymous with "overwhelm." Over the last 600 years, however, "overwhelm" has won over English speakers who have come to largely prefer it to "whelm," despite the latter's brevity. Perhaps the emphatic redundancy of "overwhelm" makes it seem like the more fitting word for describing the experience of being overcome by powerful forces or feelings.

And here are different meanings of the word *overwhelm*, also according to Merriam-Webster.com:

1. To affect (someone) very strongly. Grief *overwhelmed* her. = She was *overwhelmed* by grief. [=she felt grief so strongly that she was unable to think or act in a normal way]

2. To cause (someone) to have too many things to deal with. The many requests for assistance *overwhelmed* them. = They were *overwhelmed* by the many requests for assistance. [=they could not respond to the many requests for assistance because there were too many]

3. To defeat (someone or something) completely. The city was *overwhelmed* by the invading army.

Sheesh! I don't know about you, but after reading these descriptions, the last thing I would ever want to describe myself as is *overwhelmed*. (Of course, you could start saying that you're feeling *whelmed*, but then no one would know what you were talking about.)

Now, why have I taken so long to talk about one little word? You may be thinking, "But Noah, is this really a big deal?"

STICKS AND STONES?

We've all heard the phrase, "Sticks and stones may break my bones, but words will never hurt me." Some of us may even remember saying it when we were kids. Why? Because it's a common childhood chant that's meant to say that hurtful words cannot cause physical pain, and therefore, we're going to ignore them.

Now let me ask you a question. When you were a kid, how many times did someone throw sticks or stones at you?

Whenever I ask that question of my audiences in my keynote speeches, seminars, or private workshops, most people say, "Never. No one ever threw sticks or stones at me."

Then I ask the follow-up question: "When you were a kid, did you ever have someone hurl hurtful words at you?"

Every hand goes up.

Then I ask the key question: "How many of us still hear those hurtful words in our heads to this day?"

Nearly every hand goes up again.

So, is it true that "words will never hurt me?"

No. In fact, most of us know from painful experience that words can hurt us more deeply and for a longer period of time than anything else we encounter in life—far worse than sticks or stones ever could.

Because, while physical scars heal, emotional scars—the ones formed by hurtful words—often don't heal, ever. That means that whether you're old or young, for better or worse, for richer or poorer, *words* are the building blocks of your emotional life.

WORDS CAN HURT US MORE DEEPLY THAN STICKS AND STONES EVER COULD.

WHAT ARE YOU THINKING?

Think about it.

What are you thinking right now?

Whatever you're thinking, you are using *words* to think with. Now, you might say, "Well, duh, Noah. I think I knew that I was using words to think with. What else am I going to think with?"

Exactly! What else *are* you going to think with?

That's why I say that words are the building blocks of your emotional life. But what does that mean, how does it affect you, and what can you do about it?

WORDS ARE THE BUILDING BLOCKS OF YOUR EMOTIONAL LIFE.

To answer that question, let's look at two different people and examine how they do something very simple called *get up in the morning*.

Since we're about to embark on an excellent adventure, let's call our two people Bill and Ted. (All of you movie nerds will get that 1980s reference.) And since I just brought up the movies, imagine that you're watching a movie right now. The opening scene is Bill's bedroom first thing in the morning, and the second scene is Ted's bedroom first thing in the morning.

Our opening shot is looking into Bill's bedroom. We see Bill tossing and turning in his bed. We get a sense that he had a fitful night of not enough sleep. His face is contorted as if in some kind of pain or fear.

We hear Bill's alarm going off. He groans, turns over, and hits the snooze button. Now we hear his thoughts in a voiceover: "Aw, crap. Not this again. I don't wanna get out of bed. It's too early. I hate my job; I hate my boss; I hate my life. What's the point, anyway?"

Now let's zoom out of our movie for a moment and think about this. Imagine that Bill is a real person who has those thoughts, those words running through his head first thing in the morning, each and every morning when he wakes up.

How do you think Bill's morning is going to go if he's thinking those thoughts? How's his day going to go if those are the words he's saying to himself? How's his *life* going to go if he keeps saying those things to himself day after day?

Now, let's go back into our movie of the imagination. In the next scene, we are looking into Ted's bedroom. We see Ted sleeping peacefully, a smile on his face. He's clearly having sweet dreams. We're expecting the alarm to go off . . . when suddenly, Ted opens his eyes without even needing the alarm. He looks at the clock on his nightstand and smiles.

Now we hear Ted's thoughts in a voiceover: "Another beautiful day! What a great day to be alive. I'm so grateful I get to do what I do with the people I enjoy working with. This is going to be a great day!"

Now let's zoom out of our movie again and consider this. Imagine that Ted is another real person who has those words running through his head the first thing in the morning.

How do you think Ted's morning is going to go if he's thinking those thoughts? How's his day going to go if those are the words he's saying to himself? How's his *life* going to go if he keeps saying those things to himself day after day?

And now for the key question: Which set of thoughts can you relate to most of the time—Bill's or Ted's?

Which set of thoughts sounds more like the ones you wake up with most of the time? Which set of thoughts would you like to be the ones you wake up with of the time?

WOULD YOU LIKE TO HAVE SOME OF THESE THINGS, TOO?

Yes, I'm saying most of the time because, let's face it, we're not Vulcans or androids. (Will the nerd references ever stop?) (Ah, no. They won't. Just FYI.) We're human beings who go through stuff. And yes, some days are better than others.

However, you're reading this book because you'd like to make more of your days better than most. Meaning, when things don't go your way, wouldn't it be nice to have a set of simple tools so you could turn things around quickly and easily?

And when things are going your way, wouldn't it be great to have a simple, easy method to make them even better?

Let me go out on a limb here and say that in addition to having more financial freedom and success, I'd be willing to bet that you also want some, if not all, of these other things, too:

- Stop putting so much pressure on yourself.
- Stop comparing yourself to others.
- Stop missing the goals you set for yourself.
- Feel less stressed.
- Be more in control of your day.
- Be less affected by what other people do and don't do.
- Stop feeling exhausted, depressed, resentful, and overwhelmed.

Would you agree? If so, here's what I want you to know: *Words are the key to it all.*

Although there's a chance that you're reading this book after years of being stressed about money, there's also a good chance that you're reading this book in the early stages of your life and work journey, which means that you simply may be feeling a little overwhelmed and looking for answers.

FOLLOWING MY AFFORMATIONS METHOD WILL CHANGE THE TRAJECTORY OF YOUR LIFE FOR GOOD.

If that's the case, then following my Afformations Method every day will be one of the most important things you can do to change the trajectory of your personal and professional life for good.

The good news is, it's worth it! And it can **also be** even more fun and far more rewarding than you might imagine.

In this book, I'm going to teach you a revolutionary way to use words in a way that you've probably never considered before. However, before I get into exactly *how* you can master your words, let me make a case for *why*. Because, believe me, once you've uncovered the profound truth about your words, you'll never want to go back to the old way of thinking.

WHY DO WORDS MATTER SO MUCH?

As I have just shown you, the more you understand the power of your words, the more you'll realize that harnessing that power will give you tremendous advantages in life and work. In fact, once you start harnessing the awesome power of your words using my Afformations Method, you can expect to enjoy these important and valuable benefits.

YOU'LL MAKE MORE MONEY.

GATES, BRANSON, AND BUFFETT AGREE THAT THIS IS THE MOST IMPORTANT SKILL YOU CAN MASTER.

If Bill Gates, Richard Branson, and Warren Buffett all say that in order to be successful, there's one skill above all others that's the most important, would you pay attention? I certainly hope so!

Here's Bill Gates in a BBC News interview: "Communication skills are very important when it comes to success."

Here's Richard Branson on his own Virgin blog: "Communication makes the world go round. It facilitates human connections and allows us to learn, grow, and progress. It's not just about speaking or reading but understanding what is being said—and in some cases, what is not being said. Communication is the most important skill any leader can possess."

And here's Warren Buffett talking to a Stanford MBA graduate student: "At your age, the best way you can improve yourself is to learn to communicate better. Your results in life will be magnified if you can communicate them better. The only diploma I hang in my office is the communications diploma I got from Dale Carnegie in 1952."

Buffett continues: "Without good communication skills, you won't be able to convince people to follow you, even though you see over the mountain and they don't."

Three billionaires, one skill. Case closed.

But wait, there's more!

YOU'LL BE HAPPIER.

Have you heard the phrase, "Happy wife, happy life?" Or the more encompassing: "Happy spouse, happy house?" According to a scientific study on the causes of divorce done by the National Institutes of Health, 72% of divorced couples cite "too much conflict and arguing" as a major contributor to divorce.

Respondents in the study also reported that such communication problems increased in frequency and intensity over the course of their marriages.

USING THE RIGHT WORDS PLAYS A CRUCIAL ROLE IN YOUR MENTAL HEALTH AND HAPPINESS.

In addition, researcher John Gottman, who has conducted relationship studies for over forty years at the University of Washington, has concluded that the one thing couples struggle the most with is effectively communicating with one another in a relationship.

Since the not-surprising statistics show that divorced individuals, compared to their married counterparts, have higher levels of psychological distress, substance abuse, and depression, as well as lower levels of overall health, it's clear that using the right words (and eliminating the *wrong* words) plays an enormous role in your mental health, happiness, and wellness over the course of your lifetime.

YOU'LL BE HEALTHIER.

According to the National Institutes of Health, several recent studies have discovered numerous positive associations between communication skills and improved health, including lower blood pressure, fewer headaches, and lower depression.

Also, did you read a few paragraphs ago when I said that better communication skills will help you have a happier marriage?

I don't know about you, but I've been in plenty of unhealthy relationships where trying to communicate with the other person made me physically ill. However, now that I've cleaned up my communication skills and cleared out all the negative people from my relationships by following my own Afformations Method, I'm happier and healthier than I've been in my entire life. You should try it!

YOU'LL HAVE HIGHER SELF-ESTEEM.

With better communication comes higher self-esteem. According to Healthfully.com, people with high self-esteem tend to have better communication skills—whereas people with low self-esteem have a harder time communicating with others, making it harder for them to develop healthy relationships, thereby lowering their self-esteem even further.

TO IMPROVE YOUR SELF-ESTEEM, IMPROVE YOUR COMMUNICATION SKILLS.

I can certainly confirm this. Throughout high school and college, even into my late twenties, I had such low self-esteem that I could barely look people in the eye. I walked around with my shoulders slumped over, and I would hardly speak to other people—and when I did, I usually mumbled no more than a few words.

Contrast that to today when it's hard to get me to shut up! (Just ask my wife.) My shoulders are back, I look people in the eye, and I have healthier self-esteem than at any time before.

There's no doubt that for me, the key to making this life-changing transformation was discovering how to harness the power of words.

YOU'LL BE PERCEIVED BY OTHERS AS A LEADER.

A study on entrepreneurship published by the *American Journal of Small Business* showed that among both small business owners and bank loan representatives, the top-ranked characteristics among successful entrepreneurs were oral communication and listening.

Think about leaders in all walks of life—from business to politics to health. Can you think of one highly successful person in any field who isn't a great communicator? I sure can't.

That's yet another reason that, when you discover how to harness the power of your words, you'll be perceived by others—your peers, colleagues, customers, even people who can loan you money—as a leader, someone who knows where they're going and how to get there.

The old saying is true: "The world loves a person with a plan."

YOU'LL MAKE *A LOT* MORE MONEY.

Did I mention that before?

See Gates, Buffett, Branson, et al.

Bottom line: The experts have weighed in, and the data are clear. *When you discover how to master the power of your words, your life will change forever.*

CHANGE MY BELIEFS? REALLY?

YOU CAN CHANGE YOUR BELIEFS IN THE NEXT 14 DAYS IF YOU DO THIS.

It's true. Changing your beliefs from the ones you're holding right now means going from being barely aware of what you're thinking most of the time to being more aware of what you're thinking most of the time to being fully aware of what you're thinking *almost all the time.*

Like any new habit, this is a process. However, if you follow the exercises and recommendations I give you in this book, I will help you go from *barely aware* to *more aware* to *fully aware* in the next fourteen days or less.

Big promise? You bet! Yet this isn't some pie-in-the-sky, positive thinking, woo-woo stuff. That's because, after more than a quarter-century of helping over a million people just like you from around the world to harness the power of words, I know from personal experience that it cannot only happen, it's a solid guarantee—provided you follow the steps.

That means more than a million people around the planet are already following my Afformations Method to improve every aspect of their lives—from health to wealth to relationships to creating the lives of their dreams.

Furthermore, many of them, prior to following my Afformations Method, had already tried lots of other personal development techniques without seeing many, if any, results.

What this means for you is that whether you've been at this personal growth game for a while or you're just getting started, the benefits of harnessing the power of your words will pay you great dividends over the coming months and years.

Still skeptical? Then let me tell you this: *The hardest part about changing your words is becoming aware of the words you're already using right now.*

WHEN YOU RULE YOUR WORDS, YOU RULE YOUR WORLD.

That's because you've probably been thinking the words you've been thinking and saying to yourself for years or even decades. That means those thoughts, those words, those beliefs you've been holding on to have become *unconscious*— which means that you're not even aware you're holding on to them.

That's why becoming aware is the starting point for *Millionaire AFFORMATIONS*. Yes, it's time for you to harness the awesome power of your words—because when you rule your words, you rule your world.

In the next two chapters, I'll show you how to harness the tremendous power of your words, whether you've never read a self-help book in your life or you're a self-help junkie who's been to every personal growth seminar on the planet.

I'll also reveal the four 'A's of my AFFORMATIONS® Method and show you how to harness the life-changing magic of the most powerful and effective belief-change method ever discovered.

In chapters 5 through 12, I give you my 301 favorite Millionaire Afformations, which are guaranteed to empower you to experience greater success in every area of your life. This section also includes stories from real-life Afformers like you, who followed my 14-Day Millionaire Afformations Sprint and achieved remarkable results.

Chapter 13 covers "The ABCs" of Making a Millionaire and gives you the tools you must master to become a millionaire, whether you're just starting out or you've been working on it for a long time.

In chapter 14, I reveal my 14-Day Millionaire Afformations Sprint so you can jump-start your Afformation habit, which will help you achieve extraordinary results faster than you ever thought possible.

We have a lot of ground to cover in this book, so *let's go!*

- 2 -

IT ONLY TAKES FIVE MINUTES A DAY TO CHANGE YOUR LIFE

"If one can't answer, simplify the question."

— TOBA BETA

Now you understand why the words you say to yourself are the single most important factor in determining your level of success (or non-success) in life and business. However, just because you understand *why* something is important doesn't mean you know *what* to do or *how* to do it yet.

As we saw with our movie of the imagination exercise from the previous chapter, there are essentially only two ways to go through the days of our lives—like Bill or like Ted.

To help you remember which one you'd rather be, I came up with these helpful acronyms: GEAR and FAR. GEAR stands for going through life feeling *Grateful, Excited, Appreciative,* and *Relaxed,* while FAR stands for going through life *Fearful, Angry,* and *Resentful.*

So, which would you rather be: GEAR (Ted's story) or FAR (Bill's story)? The answer should be incredibly obvious.

(Also, sorry that I couldn't use the acronym NEAR instead of GEAR, but the closest synonym to Gratitude that starts with the letter N is *nirvanic,* which didn't quite fit.)

What if, like so many people today, you really do feel FAR from your goals much of the time—Fearful, Angry, and Resentful? What if you're feeling FAR right now but really do want to get in GEAR? (Hey, that did work out!)

In other words, how do we go from FAR to GEAR?

The good news is that it is possible to go from FAR to GEAR—even if you've spent most of your life feeling FAR from your goals (wow, these acronyms are really working).

THIS IS HOW WE GO FROM FAR TO GEAR.

Sound too good to be true?

You may be thinking, *Sure Noah, that might be true for some people, those Pollyannas with fake smiles plastered on their faces. But I'm a realist. I know that there's a lot to be afraid of, and I don't trust people who look on the bright side all the time.*

Yet I know from personal experience that you can go from feeling FAR from your goals to getting in GEAR, even when you don't think you can do it.

How do I know? Because I used to be as FAR from my goals as you can possibly imagine. Yet today, I've created the life and business of my dreams by following the method I'm giving you in this book.

You see, the raw, unfiltered truth is that my struggles began in high school. In fact, I was the classic "nerd" with Coke-bottle glasses, a face full of acne, and shoulder-width (not shoulder-length) hair.

I tried in vain to get the self-confidence to believe in myself and pursue my dreams. I read every self-help book out there, hoping to find "the answer." But I just ended up more frustrated than before.

Eventually, at age twenty-five, I was so depressed and frustrated, I decided to commit suicide. When my life was spared at the last moment, I decided to go on a quest to discover "the missing piece" that none of those self-help books or "experts" ever talk about.

Amazingly, after years and years of painful searching, I finally found it. That was how it started . . . and now? I'm living a life that's fulfilled in ways I never dreamed possible.

That's the key message about changing your beliefs—you CAN do it. Even though most people may not be born *Grateful, Excited, Appreciative,* and *Relaxed,* you can train yourself to be.

If I can do it, anyone can—and it doesn't require a supreme act of willpower or pretending to be something you're not.

In fact, as I've seen through my own experience and that of my coaching clients, changing your beliefs is not just something you can do; it can also become a fundamental part of *who you are* and that you will love and enjoy this New You.

IF I CAN DO IT, ANYONE CAN.

Still not convinced? Then suspend your disbelief for a moment and let me introduce you to the four-step process that changed my life—four simple, foolproof steps that made changing my beliefs from negative to positive easier than I ever thought possible.

In fact, if I hadn't discovered this method, I honestly don't know if I would still be alive.

THE CHALLENGE OF CHANGING YOUR BELIEFS

Changing your beliefs is not like changing your clothes or changing the sheets on your bed. That's because, unlike our clothes or bed sheets, most of us presume that our beliefs are hard-wired into us. Indeed, I would go so far as to say that most people believe they *are* their beliefs.

For example, let's say you grew up in New England, and for your whole life, the people you grew up with followed the Boston Red Sox. (I know I may have just lost a lot of my New York readers, but please stay with me here. Remember, *this is just an example. Use whatever sports team you want.*)

So here you are, growing up with the belief, *I'm a Red Sox fan.* You watch Red Sox games, root for them, cheer when they win, and hurt when they lose.

Then one day, you hear the comedian Jerry Seinfeld do his routine where he realized that when you're a sports fan, you root for a team, yet any player on that team can be traded to any other team at any time.

So, what, exactly, are you rooting for? According to Seinfeld, since any player can switch one team's uniform for another team's uniform at any time, when you're rooting for a team, *you're actually rooting for the laundry.*

You hear that and think to yourself: *You know what, he's right. I am rooting for the laundry.* If you think about it, there's no such thing as the Boston Red Sox. There's only this *idea* of a *thing* called the Boston Red Sox, that is, in essence, laundry.

I remember when I heard Seinfeld say that, at first, I was taken aback. Because, like any good boy who grew up in New England, I was indeed a die-hard Red Sox fan.

However, the more I thought about it, I realized that Jerry was right. For instance, what happens when you root for a player one day, and the next day they're playing for the opposing team? Who or what, exactly, are you rooting for?

MOST PEOPLE BELIEVE THEY ARE THEIR BELIEFS.

That is a simple but perhaps profound example of what it means and what it takes to change our beliefs. Before becoming aware of the fact that (for example) a sports team is nothing more than an *idea*, you may have spent a lot of time, money, and emotion following and rooting for that team.

But now you're like, *What am I getting so worked up about?*

That is an example of how your beliefs can change when you *change your perspective.* Have you ever noticed that it often takes an objective third party to give us that new perspective?

Therefore, when you follow the simple step-by-step method that you're about to discover, in a few weeks (maybe even a few days), you'll be saying to yourself, *Wow! Now I know how to change my beliefs—and it wasn't as hard as I thought it would be!*

YES, YOU CAN CHANGE YOUR LIFE IN JUST FIVE MINUTES A DAY

In the next chapter, I'm going to reveal my AFFORMATIONS® Method—the legendary process that has empowered over a million people around the world to change their lives for the better.

YOUR BELIEFS CHANGE WHEN YOU CHANGE YOUR PERSPECTIVE.

Every day, my inbox is filled with emails from grateful customers from across the globe who share their transformational success stories with me. In fact, in this book, I'll share some of their real-life Afformations success stories with you.

Yet, as we begin this process, I want you to know that the most important step to changing your beliefs is to *identify the reasons why* you want to make these changes in the first place.

Everything we do, every behavior, every action, every step we take is determined by what I call our Why-To's. As I often say, "When you find your Why, you'll find the Way."

Let me tell you a story to illustrate this point.

When I launched SuccessClinic.com in 1997, I was a thirty-year-old religious studies major living in a 300-square-foot basement apartment. I had less than $800 in my bank account. I had no money, no connections, no marketing skills, no sales experience, no business acumen, and no idea how to run a successful online business.

(Keep in mind that just five years earlier, I had decided to commit suicide.)

Yet even at the very beginning, I did have the one thing that made the words you're reading right now possible—a deep, burning desire to make a difference in the lives of millions of people around the world.

Keep in mind: I had no idea *how* I would do it. I just knew I was going to do it, no matter what.

So, you would think that it was smooth sailing after that, right? Not exactly!

Instead, I ended up spending a lot of money on and trusting several unscrupulous people who took me in a lot of bad directions and caused me to lose focus on my primary mission—to make a global impact and help people around the world.

WHEN YOU FIND YOUR WHY, YOU'LL FIND THE WAY.

As a result of following their bad advice, in 2007, after ten long years of hard work and sacrifice, I ended up $40,000 in debt and had to move back into my parents' house at the age of forty.

Try that on for size—starting your company in one basement with nothing; then, ten years later, ending up in *another* basement with *less* than nothing!

Clearly, something was very wrong with what I was doing. In short, even though I was teaching people how to improve their lives, I was clearly not following my own advice! Instead, I followed a lot of "gurus" who took me and my business in a lot of wrong directions.

One day, while working in that second basement, I had a blinding flash of the obvious. I realized that not only wasn't I following my own advice, I was also letting other people tell me what direction to take my company and not being true to my original mission.

That's when I went back to my original, foundational Why-To—make a global impact and help people around the world. It was also at that time that I decided to hire my first real business coach because I knew that if I kept doing the same thing (listening to the gurus), I was going to keep getting the same results.

Keep in mind that this coach was very expensive, and I didn't have any money (i.e., I was $40,000 in debt)!

Yet, I realized then what I'm telling you now: *When you find your Why, you'll find the Way.*

So even though I didn't have the money, I *found* the money. I knew that if I didn't do this one thing that scared me—investing in this coach—I would have to give up on my dream of having a global impact and making a real difference.

What happened next changed everything.

☑ In 30 days, I launched my first online course.

☑ In 60 days, I made enough money to move out of my parents' house to an apartment in Ohio.

☑ In 90 days, I met the woman who would become my wife.

☑ In 120 days, I started getting booked to speak at seminars and conferences around the world.

Over the next few years, I was able to achieve these goals and more:

☑ Landed a six-figure deal from one of the world's largest and most prestigious publishing houses.

☑ Became the only author in history to have works published by Hay House, HarperCollins, Simon & Schuster, Mindvalley, Nightingale-Conant, and the *Chicken Soup for the Soul* publisher, with my books currently published in eighteen languages.

☑ Mentor and coach Hollywood celebrities, 8-figure CEOs, professional athletes, and elite entrepreneurs from around the world.

☑ Became known as "The Mental Health Coach to The Stars."

☑ Interviewed in over 1,000 media outlets, including ABC, NBC, CBS, FOX, The Hallmark Channel, *Entrepreneur*, *SUCCESS* magazine, and many more.

☑ Purchased my dream home—a 6,000-square-foot mansion on a hill that my clients lovingly call "Success Manor"—and paid off the mortgage 28 years early.

Noah in front of Success Manor

Today, I'm privileged to live a semi-retired lifestyle where I coach a select group of celebrities, CEOs, athletes, and entrepreneurs, so they too can have greater impact, influence and income, while enjoying more time off and getting to spend more time with their families and doing what they love.

WHAT THIS MEANS FOR YOU

Now you might be saying, "That's great, Noah—but what does this have to do with me?"

My intention for sharing my story is simple. It's to demonstrate that if someone like me—a shy, introverted nerd from Maine who was suicidal at age twenty-five and started his business at age thirty with nothing but a dream—can change my life by following this method, then you can too.

THREE SUCCESS TIPS FOR YOU

As we get ready to jump into The Four Steps of my AFFORMATIONS® Method, let me give you three quick success tips that will accelerate your results.

STEP ONE: IDENTIFY YOUR WHY-TO'S.

My story demonstrates the truth of the statement: *When you find your Why, you'll find the Way.*

However, the flip side of that statement means that if you don't understand or identify why you're doing this, you'll probably (definitely) give up when things get tough or don't go your way.

IF YOU DON'T FIND YOUR WHY, YOU'LL QUIT WHEN THINGS GET TOUGH.

Was I tempted to give up when I ended up $40,000 in debt and had to move back into my parents' house at age forty? You might think so.

However, the truth is, I knew that I would *never* give up. Not until I had exhausted **every** possible resource (or my last breath, whichever came first).

As lousy as that situation was, I knew I would find a way to succeed, whatever it took. And it was that Why-To that gave me the courage to hire that business coach against all odds and against even what was "possible" for me at the time.

So, what does this mean for *you*?

Right now, I want you to write a list of ten reasons *why* you're going to learn how to use my Afformations Method and *why* you're going to keep taking action until you see the results you want—even in the face of resistance, whether internal (from yourself) or external (from the world).

STEP TWO: SUBSCRIBE TO WATCHNOAHTV.COM.

Subscribe to my YouTube channel at WatchNoahTV.com so you can discover my latest insights and best practices on Inner Game and Outer Game Mastery and how to live a 7-Figure Life.

STEP THREE: FIND YOUR AFFORMATIONS ACCOUNTABILITY PARTNER.

Find your Afformation accountability partner—your spouse, a friend, a family member, or one of our Power Habits® Certified Coaches—to join you on this adventure so you can encourage, support, and hold each other accountable to follow through until your Afformations practice has become a lifelong habit.

Okay, now let's discover how to harness the life-changing magic of the most powerful and effective belief-change method ever discovered, which is guaranteed to empower you to embrace success in every area of your life!

- 3 -

HOW I DISCOVERED AFFORMATIONS®

"I don't pretend to have all the answers.
But the questions are certainly worth thinking about."

— ARTHUR C. CLARKE

Whether you want to make more money in your current career or start, grow, or scale your own business, you may have tried many different things to achieve those outcomes. For example, you may have tried things like . . .

- Reading self-help books.
- Listening to self-improvement audio programs.
- Attending personal growth seminars.
- Writing your goals.
- Making vision boards.
- Using "affirmations."

Wait a minute—what's that last one?

Millions of people have tried using affirmations to change their lives. Why? Because that's what the gurus told us to do!

So, do affirmations actually work? The answer, for millions of us, is, "*Meh.*"

Meaning, they sort of do and sort of don't.

Let me ask you a question. If someone gave you a phone that sometimes worked and often didn't, would you keep using that phone? Or would you trade in that phone for a better one—one that works every time?

HOW YOUR MIND WORKS

Here's a partial list of the things your mind can do, from A-Z:

Arrange, believe, create, design, engineer, form, generate, hypothesize, imagine, judge, know, lead, mastermind, notice, originate, plan, query, realize, shape, think, understand, visualize, wonder, xfer (yes, that's a word), yearn, zigzag.

Yes, the human mind can do all these things before you've even had breakfast.

In fact, the human mind has created every work of art, poetry, science, religion, philosophy, mathematics, history, and romance that has ever existed.

One way to look at your mind is that your thoughts are like seeds you plant every minute of every day of your life, whether you're aware of it or not.

Those thought-seeds are planted in the fertile soil we could call Infinite Intelligence, the Universe, or God—something greater than ourselves that takes the *thought-seeds* you plant and produces the results we call Your Life.

THE THOUGHT-SEEDS YOU PLANT BECOME YOUR LIFE.

HOW THE "GURUS" FAILED US

How many self-help books have you read that tell you to use affirmations? Probably all of them, except this one (and my other books)!

Why? Because the gurus have been telling us for decades to use affirmations.

Since self-help books have been around forever, and since the gurus all say the same thing, and since millions of people have been reading all these books that all say the same thing, you would think that by now, everyone who's ever read a self-help book would have everything they want.

Yet, we know that is not the case. And why have all those books and gurus been saying the same thing forever? The answer is, before I discovered AFFORMATIONS in April 1997, no one had ever thought to do it any other way.

THIS IS ONE OF THE BIGGEST WAYS THE GURUS FAILED US.

For example, in my keynote speeches and private workshops, I like to play a little game with my audience to see if the old way—the affirmations way—works or not.

I begin by saying, "Okay, everyone, let's start by saying a classic affirmation that the gurus have been telling us to say forever. Everyone say, "I am rich!"

Everyone says, *"I am rich!"*

"Put some emotion into it," I say.

"I am rich!" they shout with emotion.

Do you know what happens next?

Everyone starts laughing!

So, I ask them, "What are you laughing at?"

They say, "Well, I'm not rich."

I say, "But you just said you were."

And they say, "Yeah, but I don't believe it!"

THEREIN LIES THE PROBLEM

Aha! That right there is the problem. The plain and simple truth is that for many of us, we *say* those affirmations just like they told us to do . . . but we simply don't believe them.

Why don't we believe them? *Because we're trying to convince ourselves of something that isn't true.*

Of course, the gurus have said over and over that if you don't believe your affirmations, you just have to repeat them over and over, a million kajillion times . . . until, eventually, you'll believe them.

STOP TRYING TO CONVINCE YOURSELF OF SOMETHING YOU DON'T BELIEVE.

That is basically like them saying to you, "We know this phone doesn't work right now, but just keep using it, and eventually, it should work!" (Interestingly, they say this while running for the exits.)

YOUR PROBLEMS ARE REALLY JUST QUESTIONS

Now let's talk about solving problems, because that's one reason you're reading this book right now—to solve one or more problem you're facing. Whether it's money problems, health problems, relationship problems, or stress problems, any problem—from the trivial to the tremendous—is simply *a question searching for an answer*. For example, here are a few serious global problems and their associated questions:

Global warming: "How can we stop destroying Earth and still live the lives we want?"

Poverty: "How can we empower everyone in the world so nobody has to go without the basic necessities of life?"

Unemployment: "How can we get people to work in jobs that produce wealth for themselves and help society function better as well?"

(Notice I didn't say these were easy questions. That's why we haven't found all the answers yet!)

If those are serious global problems and their associated questions, what about personal problems we might face daily?

Lack of success: "How can I be more successful in my life and business?"

Lack of organization: "Why can't I find what I'm looking for?"

Lack of companionship: "Why can't I get a date on Saturday night?"

Lack of health: "How can I lose weight and be healthier?"

As you can see, many of our problems can be stated as a form of lack (i.e., "I don't have something that I want, like money, success, health, or love.").

Now, to combat that lack in your life, you **may** have tried using affirmations like they told you to. Maybe it worked for you, and maybe it didn't.

However, if you're like most people I've spoken to or coached over the last quarter-century, I could tell you that if the old method worked for you in the way you wanted, you wouldn't be reading this book right now.

That brings us to the key question:

MOST HUMAN PROBLEMS ARE SOME FORM OF LACK.

*Rather than making statements you may not believe, why not **ask questions** that will transform your life?*

THE SHOWER THAT CHANGED EVERYTHING

I was in the shower on April 24, 1997, when I discovered the Afformations Method that I'm sharing with you in this book and the other books in my AFFORMATIONS® Series. If you'd like the complete story, please read *The Book of AFFORMATIONS®* published by Hay House.

For our purposes here, it will suffice to say that the gurus have been telling us forever that the only way to change our beliefs and our lives is to change the statements we were saying to ourselves (i.e., use affirmations).

However, in The Shower That Changed Everything, I had a *life-changing epiphany* when I realized they had left out half of the equation.

When you use both parts of the equation, you will become fundamentally unstoppable.

Here's what I mean. Your mind has what I call an *Automatic Search Function*, which means that when you ask a question, your mind automatically begins to search for the answer. Psychologists have referred to it as the "embedded presupposition factor" of the brain.

USING AFFORMATIONS WILL MAKE YOU FUNDAMENTALLY UNSTOPPABLE.

For example, let's go back to Bill from our movie of the imagination. Right now, when Bill wakes up in the morning, he's focusing on everything that's wrong in his life. When he's focused on everything that's *wrong* in his life, what will he find more of? Exactly: things that are wrong in his life!

Now, look at what Ted does when he wakes up in the morning. Unlike Bill, Ted begins his day by focusing on the things that are right in his life. When he's focusing on everything that's *right* in his life, what do you think he's going to find more of? Correct: things that are right in his life.

The question is, which would you rather find: what's wrong with your life, or what's right with your life?

WHAT YOU FOCUS ON, GROWS

This all sounds great, but the question remains: How, exactly, are we supposed to change our focus from what's wrong with our lives to what's right with our lives? Are we supposed to just ignore everything that's wrong and pretend everything's fine when it really isn't?

The gurus told us that we have to change our beliefs if we want to change our lives. (At least they got that part right.) So, they told us to change the statements we were making (i.e., use affirmations).

However, they completely ignored how to harness the miraculous power of changing the *questions* we're asking. That leads to the essence of my discovery in the shower that April morning in 1997:

*If you only change the **statements** you say without changing the **questions** you ask, you're missing out on the simplest and most powerful way to change your life that's ever been discovered!*

DISEMPOWERING QUESTIONS VS. EMPOWERING QUESTIONS

There are only two kinds of questions we can ask ourselves when it comes to changing our beliefs: *disempowering* questions and *empowering* questions.

What does this mean? Let's start by examining disempowering questions—because they're the kind you may be the most familiar with, and they're also the ones you want to stop asking yourself immediately.

Disempowering questions do exactly as their name implies: they *take away your power to act*. Here are a few examples of common disempowering questions:

⇨ Why am I so stupid?

⇨ Why am I so fat?

⇨ Why can't I do anything right?

⇨ Why am I so scared?

⇨ Why doesn't anyone love me?

⇨ How come I never get the breaks other people get?

⇨ Why is there always more *month* left at the end of the *money*?

When you ask lousy questions, what do you get? Exactly: lousy answers . . . and that creates a lousy *life!*

ASK LOUSY QUESTIONS AND YOU'LL CREATE A LOUSY LIFE.

As I explain in my keynote speeches and private workshops, most of us are unconsciously carrying around what I call a **Negative Reflection**. Your *Negative Reflection* is that voice in your head that talks to you in disempowering questions like the ones I just listed.

When we ask ourselves negative disempowering questions like these, we end up creating, manifesting, and attracting what we're focusing on due to the very fact that we're asking these lousy questions.

In other words, what you focus on, grows—and when you're asking negative questions, you're going to manifest negative results.

Because these disempowering questions and your Negative Reflection tend to thrive in secret (meaning, we typically don't share these types of thoughts with other people), I'd like you to write down the five disempowering questions that you hear from your Negative Reflection most often.

Yes, I mean right now.

No matter how long you've been asking yourself these disempowering questions, it's crucial that you identify them now so we can transform them using my Afformations Method.

Write today's date next to your questions so that when you come back to this book later, you'll see just how far you've come in a very short time.

Please do this exercise right now. I'll be right here when you get back.

THE FIVE DISEMPOWERING QUESTIONS I HEAR MOST OFTEN:

1.

2.

3.

4.

5.

Now, take a deep breath, because I'm about to change your life . . .

EMPOWERING QUESTIONS—THE FOUNDATION OF YOUR NEW LIFE

Now that you've identified your most commonly asked disempowering questions, you may be saying, "Okay, Noah, now that I know my disempowering questions, can we get to *empowering* questions so I can turn this thing around?"

Absolutely!

If disempowering questions focus your mind on what you can't do, empowering questions do exactly the opposite—they empower you to focus on what you can do.

That's because the answers to empowering questions produce feelings of self-confidence, self-esteem, inner peace, and a positive self-image.

In other words, empowering questions lead to answers that tell the truth about Who You Really Are.

So, now, I want you to take the five disempowering questions you identified in the previous exercise and flip them from negative to positive.

AFFORMATIONS EMPOWER YOU TO BE WHO YOU REALLY ARE.

For example, if one of your disempowering questions was, "Why am I so stupid?" your empowering question can be, "Why am I so smart?"

If one of your disempowering questions was, "Why am I so broke?" your empowering question can be, "Why am I so rich?"

Don't worry if you don't believe your new empowering questions yet. Trust me, we're getting there!

Okay, go ahead and do this exercise right now.

THE FIVE NEW EMPOWERING QUESTIONS I'M GOING TO START ASKING:

1.

2.

3.

4.

5.

Did you notice something begin to shift in your mind?

Fantastic! Because we've just begun an amazing journey to your new life . . .

AFFORMATIONS®: THE FOUNDATION OF YOUR NEW LIFE

As you're starting to see, our lives are formed by the questions we ask ourselves. Therefore, when you repeatedly ask yourself a question, *your mind will continually search for answers to that question.*

For example, if you're constantly asking yourself disempowering questions like, "Why am I so stupid?" or "Why am I so broke?" your life will become a reflection of those questions, and you'll constantly feel stupid and broke.

I know this all too well, because these are exactly the kind of disempowering questions I had been asking myself for my entire life—until I discovered The Afformations Method in 1997 when I was thirty years old.

That means I had *nearly three decades* of asking myself lousy, disempowering questions. If someone had told me how powerful those questions were and how to change them from negative to positive, it would have changed the course of my life.

THIS IS HOW I INVENTED THE WORD AFFORMATIONS.

Of course, no one did that. It was only because I discovered The Afformations Method in The Shower That Changed Everything that I **was** able to acquire the knowledge, skills and experience **to** go from being a broke, lonely guy living in a 300-square-foot basement apartment to a happily married man living in a 6,000-square-foot mansion on a hill!

Since I'm the person who discovered The Afformations® Method, you may be asking, "Noah, where did the word *AFFORMATIONS* come from?"

I'm glad you asked! (See, you're really starting to get this!)

After my discovery in The Shower That Changed Everything, I realized that the method I had identified to change a person's disempowering questions to empowering questions could truly revolutionize the field of self-help and personal development. (That's why so many of my colleagues in the industry subscribe to my method today.)

However, I also realized that I had to come up with a simple, memorable name to express this method—so people could fully grasp how powerful this method is.

So, I went back to my roots to discover the answer. In high school, the study of Latin was one of my favorite subjects. (Why do you think they call me "the nerdiest nerd in the personal growth industry?")

I realized that the word "affirmation"—you know, the old method that the gurus have been telling us to do for decades—comes from the Latin word *firmare*, which means "to make firm."

So, I asked myself: *If affirmations are positive* statements, *what would be the perfect word to describe empowering* questions?

And the answer came to me (of course!).

I realized that when we're asking questions, what we're doing is *forming* thought patterns, which *form* our beliefs and *form* our very lives.

The word "form" comes from the Latin word *formare*, which means "to give shape to."

That's when it hit me: What if you're making something *firm* . . . but it's in the wrong *form*?

WHAT IF YOU'RE MAKING SOMETHING FIRM, BUT IT'S IN THE WRONG FORM?

At that moment, I realized why affirmations don't work very well when we're trying to change our lives. It's because we're trying to make something *firm* before we've *formed* what we want.

I also realized that instead of trying to make something *firm* that we don't believe yet, we first need to *form* questions that change the thought-seeds we're sowing, which would then empower us to change our lives.

And that's how I created the name *The AFFORMATIONS® Method.*

Now, rather than trying to make something *firm* that you don't yet believe—instead, we're going to *form* (give shape to) new beliefs in the *form* of empowering questions, which will, by definition, empower you to change your beliefs, change your habits, and change your life.

And in case you're wondering, it's perfectly legitimate to invent a new word to describe a new technology or a new way of looking at the universe.

For example, remember the first time you heard words like *Internet*, *software*, or *Google?* Even a few short years ago, these words had no meaning, because the technology they describe didn't exist. That's because there was no *context* for the words before someone came along and invented the technology that made them real. When there's no context for a word, that word has no meaning.

AFFORMATIONS ARE THE NEW TECHNOLOGY OF THE MIND.

Of course, now we use words like these every day. What didn't exist just a few years ago is now commonplace.

Since 1997, I've been teaching my clients and audience members around the world this new word that I invented—a new word to describe *a new technology of the mind.*

Hence, AFFORMATIONS: a new word to describe a new technology of the mind.

Now that you know how I invented The Afformations Method, let me give you the Four A's of my Afformations Method so you can begin to change your beliefs, change your habits, and change your life!

- 4 -

THE FOUR A'S FOR MAKING A MILLIONAIRE

"Every sentence I utter must be understood, not as an affirmation, but as a question."

— NIELS BOHR

THE FIRST A: ASK YOURSELF WHAT YOU WANT

The first A of The Afformations Method is **ASK yourself what you want**. Yes, I want you to ask yourself what you want. That means setting your goals.

Now, you might be saying: "What? I thought this was going to be different. That's the same thing every guru says!"

Yep. You're right.

Every guru does say to set your goals. But what's the very next thing they tell you to do? You're right—they tell you to use affirmations to convince yourself that you can achieve your goals.

The irony is, they had it *half* right.

True, it is very important to set goals. However, that's not the problem with what they told us. The problem with what they told us is what they told us to do *after* setting our goals.

Asking yourself what you want is like going to the grocery store. For instance, you wouldn't get in your car, drive to the grocery store, walk around the store for an hour, then get back in your car and drive home. That wouldn't make any sense!

You go to the grocery store because you want something. You might want milk, eggs, bread, butter, and whatever else is on your shopping list. The point is that you know what you want, and you know why you're going to the store.

THE PROBLEM IS WHAT THEY TOLD US TO DO AFTER WE SET GOALS.

However, did you know that millions of people don't know what they want and don't know where they're going? That means they don't have a destination. A goal is simply a destination with a deadline.

Which means, if you don't know what you want, how can you be expected to get it?

Therefore, I want you to *ask yourself what you want* when it comes to being a millionaire. Why? Because if you don't do this foundational step, you won't be able to complete the rest of The Afformations Method.

I want you to also realize something else that's very important. The gurus stopped right here!

In other words, the gurus said to set your goals and then use "affirmations" to convince yourself that you can reach your goals. The problem is that millions of us tried that old way and found that it just didn't work for us. What's worse, though, is that we thought it was our fault that we didn't reach our goals—when the truth is that it wasn't our fault, but the fault of the method we were told to use that caused us to fail.

Indeed, many of us who tried that old method honestly believed that we were the cause of the failure. I know this because so many people have told me so at my keynote speeches and seminars around the world for the last twenty-five years!

As I've continually stated over the last two decades in my private coaching groups and online courses, using the old "affirmation" method is like the gurus telling you to drive a nail into the wall—and then handing you a chainsaw!

It's not that they told us to do something wrong. They just handed us a tool that was ill-suited for the job.

That's why The Afformations Method makes reaching your goals so much faster and easier, because The Method harnesses the power of your subconscious mind using empowering questions—something the gurus never taught us.

STOP TRYING TO DRIVE A NAIL INTO THE WALL USING A CHAINSAW.

Now that you know your destination (Step 1), let's go to the second A of The Afformations Method—the key step to forming your new, happier, and richer life!

THE SECOND A: AFFORM THAT WHAT YOU WANT IS ALREADY TRUE

Now, we get to the essential difference between my Afformations Method and every other belief-change method on the planet.

Rather than trying to convince yourself that you can get what you want using the old affirmation technique, I want you to start asking yourself *why* you already have what you want using my AFFORMATION Method!

What the heck am I talking about?

Let's use a simple example. Let's say I want to make more money. That's why you're reading this book, right?

So, in The First A, you would ask yourself what you want and say (for example), "I want to make an additional $10,000 a month."

Now, for most people, an additional $10,000 a month would be life-changing money. For example, I've helped many of my coaching clients add an additional $10,000 a month (and much, much more) to their income. And they've used that money to:

✓ Buy a new house.

✓ Upgrade their wardrobe.

✓ Take their family on exotic vacations.

✓ Send their kids to the college or university of their choice.

✓ Walk into a car dealership and pick any car on the lot.

✓ Retire their spouse.

✓ Fund their retirement.

✓ Pay off their debts and live debt-free forever.

In other words, having that extra money would truly change your life for the better!

Therefore, in this example, for the Second A of my Afformations Method, you would *AFFORM* something like this:

"Why am I making an extra $10,000 a month?"

WE'RE TALKING LIFE-CHANGING MONEY HERE!

WHY THIS STEP WILL CHANGE YOUR LIFE—AND HOW

As we've seen, your life reflects the thought-seeds you continually plant in your mind. These thought-seeds are planted in two ways: by the *statements* you say to yourself and others, and by the *questions* you ask yourself and others.

As we've also seen, the gurus told you to change your statements (use affirmations) to get the things you want (reach your goals). And that sort of worked, sometimes.

However, when you do this step of The Afformations Method, you will begin to take what has been hidden in your subconscious mind and bring it to your conscious awareness.

For example, one of my first coaching clients over twenty years ago said to me, "Noah, as we're doing this work together, it's like you're turning on a light in a room that has been dark my whole life."

That's when I realized: *Wow, that's exactly what it's like!*

Think about it. Imagine you're in your home one night, and someone comes into your home and turns off all the lights. You don't have your phone or a flashlight, it's pitch-dark, and you can't see a thing.

Then they say to you, "Okay, now I want you to rearrange the furniture."

And you're like, *Ummmmmm . . .*

"What's the problem?" they ask. "Come on, think positive! Set your goals! You can do it!"

> USING AFFORMATIONS IS LIKE TURNING ON THE LIGHT IN YOUR CONSCIOUSNESS.

"All right," you say, and you start bumping your shins on the coffee table, scrambling around in the dark, and completely *failing* in your mission to rearrange the furniture.

Now I want you to notice what they're doing. They're trying to motivate you and "psych you up" using traditional motivational techniques used by the gurus.

However, what's the *real* problem here?

The real problem is, *you can't see what you're doing!*

So, here's what I do (both in my coaching and with The Afformations Method).

I come in and go, *click!*

In other words, I turn on the light in your consciousness. Which means now you can say, "Oh! There it is. Now I can do it!"

And guess what? You don't even need to motivate yourself or psych yourself up—because you can finally see everything right in front of you!

THE ONLY TWO THINGS THAT DETERMINE YOUR QUALITY OF LIFE

I was meditating one morning when I realized that the quality of any human being's life depends on just two things. Once you fully grasp the power of this truth, life becomes very simple.

Here's what I realized in my meditation:

*Your quality of life depends on just two things: the quality of your communication with the world **inside** of you, and the quality of your communication with the world **outside** of you.*

That's it. Those two things determine how rich or poor, happy or unhappy, successful or unsuccessful, loved or lonely you are—

the quality of your communication with the world inside of you and the quality of your communication with the world outside of you.

The quality of your communication with the world inside of you, I call your Inner Game.

The quality of your communication with the world outside of you, I call your Outer Game.

Here's the diagram I use to illustrate this point:

INNER GAME   OUTER GAME

INNER GAME	SUCCESS	OUTER GAME
Beliefs	S	Habits
Values	U	Lifestyle
Desires	C	Actions
Thoughts	C	Behaviors
Priorities	E	Systems
Decisions	S	Strategies
	S	

Inner Game means everything that happens between your ears that you can't see directly, but that affects everything you do and everything you experience in life.

For example, in my keynote speeches and workshops, I'll often ask my audiences, "What is one area of your life where your beliefs don't affect you?"

People think for a moment and go *uhhhh, ummmm . . .*

And I say, "Exactly! There's no area of your life where your beliefs don't affect you."

Think about it. Your beliefs affect your:

✓ Health

✓ Wealth

✓ Happiness

✓ Relationships

✓ Financial decisions

✓ Emotional well-being

✓ Peace of mind

✓ Stress level

> **TO CREATE THE LIFE YOU WANT, YOU MUST MASTER YOUR INNER GAME AND OUTER GAME.**

. . . and everything else you're going to experience in this lifetime.

By the same token, *Outer Game* means everything you *can* see directly because it's right in front of your face.

Outer Game means the things you *do* and what happens in your outside world, whereas Inner Game means how you think and what you believe about what happens to you.

It is often said that it's not what happens to us, but what we *believe* about what happens to us that makes all the difference in our lives. And I agree that's true to a great extent.

However, now that you are starting to follow my Afformations Method, you're not only going to feel a greater sense of *control* over what happens in your life, you'll also be able to *create* the experiences you want with far greater speed and accuracy than ever before!

WHY ASK WHY?

One of the most common questions I'm asked about Afformations is, "Why do Afformations start with the word *why*?" A good question, and here's the answer.

Human behavior is driven by two forces—the *why* and the *how*. The *why* is your *motive* for doing something; the *how* is your *method* of doing it. Which do you think is more powerful, the why or the how?

To answer that, let me ask you another question. Have you ever noticed that you can know *how* to do something but never actually *do* it?

For example, there are hundreds of things you could do right now that you choose not to—run down the street naked, hug a cactus, or pick a fight with Chuck Norris (please don't do any of these!).

In other words, you can know *how* to do something yet never do it—because you don't have the motive or *why* for doing it.

That's why *motive* surpasses *method*, which means *why* surpasses *how*—and that is why AFFORMATIONS start with the word *why*.

Now, there's nothing wrong with *how* questions. For instance, when you're working to accomplish a goal, you certainly need to know *how* to do it.

THIS IS WHY AFFORMATIONS START WITH THE WORD WHY.

The problem is that your mind can often get stuck on the *how* of doing something. For example, if you keep asking yourself, "How did I do this?" and "How did I do that?" it does not activate the embedded presupposition factor of your brain as Afformations do.

In short, Afformations are a specific form of empowering question that starts with the word *why*. When you ask questions that assume *what you want is already true,* you will activate the part of your brain that will seek to make it so. And that is what will unleash your hidden power to take action and change your life!

This brings us to the third A of my Afformations Method.

THE THIRD A: ACCEPT THE TRUTH OF YOUR NEW QUESTIONS

Now you might think that the next step of The Afformations Method would be to find the answer to the questions you're asking. And you'd be wrong. Here's why:

The purpose of Afformations is *not* to answer the new questions you're asking. Instead, the purpose of using Afformations is to refocus your mind on what you *have* instead of what you *lack*.

Earlier in this book, I said that your life is a reflection of the thoughts, feelings, and things you continually focus on. Or, put more simply: *What you focus on, grows.*

Let's go back to our movie of the imagination with our friends Bill and Ted. As you recall, Bill woke up in the morning with thoughts like, *I don't wanna get out of bed; I hate my job; I hate my boss; I hate my life. Why is my life so miserable?*

As you can see by his thoughts, Bill is focusing on everything that's *wrong* in his life. He was also using AFFORMATIONS, except he was using a disempowering Afformation to focus his mind in the *wrong* direction!

Now it's clear that every one of us can find something wrong with our lives without too much effort. In fact, there are numerous forces at work that promulgate this phenomenon. (Wow, that's a lot of big words for one sentence.)

Here's what I mean. When you check your social media feed today, I'll bet you can find plenty of people who are talking about things that are going great in their lives, and you'll also find plenty of people who are talking about things that are awful in their lives.

What about the national media? I've heard plenty of stories that say different wealthy individuals over the years have tried to launch a news network that focuses on positive, uplifting stories—only to find that no one wanted to watch positive news stories because positive news is boring!

That's why we get stories about kittens and puppies in the last two minutes of every newscast—so they give us that teensy shot of happiness after they just spent twenty-eight minutes showing us blood and guts.

The irony is that this very fact reflects the human brain itself. There's a tiny part of the brain called the amygdala, which is responsible for the "fight, flight, or freeze" response. Many neuroscientists believe that when information enters the brain, it passes through the amygdala for processing.

AFFORMATIONS WILL FOCUS YOUR MIND ON WHAT YOU HAVE INSTEAD OF WHAT YOU LACK.

The job of the amygdala is essentially to ask, "Is this (whatever it is) going to help me or harm me?"

The irony is, because the amygdala's main job is to keep you not dead—that is, to ward off any potential harm—millions of people today are in a constant state of "fight or flight."

This is yet another reason why so many people feel stressed out and scared most of the time. That brings us to why this is a key step of my Afformations Method.

THE FOUR MODES OF HUMAN COMMUNICATION

Human beings have developed four methods to communicate with one another. I call these The Four Modes of Human Communication—or, more simply, The Core 4.

The Core 4 are:

1. Reading
2. Writing
3. Speaking
4. Listening

That is how we humans assimilate information and communicate with each other and ourselves.

Because that's true, I want you to take the Afformations that you created in Step Two and use all four modes to assimilate this new information into your brain.

Here's how you're going to do it:

1. Reading. I want you to start reading your new Afformations, both from this book and ones that you write yourself. That's why I've given you my 301 favorite Millionaire Afformations beginning in the next section, so you can read them and incorporate them into your new thinking process.

2. Writing. Decades ago, when I began my studies of how the human mind works, I ran across the work of Catherine Ponder. In her books, she recommended writing an affirmation fifteen times to get an even faster result.

LISTEN TO IAFFORM AUDIOS ANYTIME, ANYWHERE TO CHANGE YOUR BRAIN AND CHANGE YOUR LIFE.

Now that you're discovering and going to be using my Afformations Method, you can use a similar strategy, but use this new and improved method (i.e., follow my Afformations Method instead of affirmations).

It's like the difference between building your house using a hammer or a nail gun. Both tools work, but one tool will get you a much faster result with a lot less time and effort.

Therefore, in addition to reading, I also want you to write your new Millionaire Afformations at least fifteen times to accelerate your results. I also recommend writing and doing the exercises in the Millionaire Afformations Journal, available at www.MillionaireAfformations.com.

3. Speaking. In addition to Reading and Writing, I also want you to say your new Millionaire Afformations out loud. You can say them to yourself, to your spouse, to your friends, to your dog or cat—heck, I've even had people tell me they love to sing their Afformations in the shower!

4. Listening. In addition to all the above, I also want you to listen to your new Afformations. Because listening is such a crucial communication mode, I created **iAfform**® **Audios**—downloadable digital audio recordings of some of my favorite Afformations set to inspiring music.

In fact, I created iAfform Audios in the major areas of life, including:

✓ Ultimate Wealth

✓ Ultimate Health

✓ Ultimate Love

✓ Easy Weight Loss

✓ Deep Blissful Sleep

✓ Your Life Purpose

. . . and many more!

The other wonderful thing about iAfform Audios is that because they work on the subconscious mind, you can listen to them anytime, anywhere—in your home or office, while you're working or relaxing, eating or exercising . . . *even while you sleep!*

Because iAfform Audios change your subconscious thought patterns using my Afformations Method, you can literally change your beliefs and start to change your life when you're not even paying attention.

Start your iAfform Audio collection and start listening now at **www.iAfform.com**.

That brings us to the fourth A of my Afformations Method, the most crucial one of all, and the step you must do if you truly want this method to work for you.

WHILE WE CAN'T CONTROL EVERYTHING, WE CAN CONTROL THESE THREE THINGS.

THE FOURTH A: ACT BASED ON YOUR NEW ASSUMPTIONS

Right now, you and I and every other human being are making *assumptions* about life and our relationship to it. These assumptions form the basis of how we go through life—whether we're going to be happy or unhappy, successful or unsuccessful, lonely or loved, secure or shy, self-confident or scared.

Ironically, most people don't realize that they're making these assumptions in the first place. They incorrectly assume that they're living the lives they're supposed to and that there's nothing they can do about it.

Nothing could be further from the truth!

You and I and every other human being have a *choice* about how we're going to go through life. While we often can't control what happens to us, we can control what we do about it.

Although there are many things we can't control, there are three things we can completely control:

1. What we think (our Thoughts)

2. What we say (our Words)

3. What we do (our Actions)

Thoughts, Words, Actions.

That's it. That's all we can control.

But that's enough.

NOAH'S NOTE: HERE'S WHAT I WANT YOU TO DO NOW

Step 1: Write 20 Afformations using the Afformations Method I taught you in this chapter.

Step 2: Circle the three Afformations that have the most meaning to you—the ones that jump out at you—the ones you have the most emotion around. It could even be the ones you don't believe you'll ever have.

Yes, those are the ones I want you to focus on. Because if they're hitting you emotionally, there's a good reason.

Step 3: List three *actions* you could take to make each of your top three Afformations true.

"Whaaaaa? I thought you said we didn't have to find the answers to the questions?"

Hold your horses! I did say that. In fact, if this were one of those "Law of Attraction" books, it would say something like, *Just believe, and it will come to you!*

Seriously??

Come on. We're living on planet Earth.

I don't know what planet they're talking about, where things just magically happen because we think about them and we don't have to do anything to *make* them happen. Because if I could find that planet, I'd move there tomorrow!

WE HAVE TO DO THIS ANNOYING THING CALLED TAKE ACTION IF WE WANT TO GET RESULTS.

However, on planet Earth, we must do this annoying thing called *take action* in order to get the things we want.

It's like if someone came up to me and said, "Hey Noah, I want to lose weight and have six-pack abs. So, I'm going to sit on the couch and eat junk food and think about having six-pack abs!"

And I'd go . . .

No!

As wonderful as that would be, it just doesn't work that way on planet Earth. That's why we must *take action* in order to get the things we want.

Over the last twenty-five years, I've had the privilege of mentoring and coaching people from all walks of life around the world, including:

- ✓ Hollywood celebrities
- ✓ 7- and 8-figure company CEOs
- ✓ Professional athletes
- ✓ Elite entrepreneurs
- ✓ Wealth managers
- ✓ Financial planners
- ✓ Real estate professionals
- ✓ B2B consultants
- ✓ Health professionals

- ✓ Chiropractors
- ✓ Network marketers
- ✓ Affiliate marketers
- ✓ Online marketers
- ✓ Coaches
- ✓ Authors
- ✓ Artists
- ✓ Service providers

. . . and many, many more.

And in all that time, I've never had a single client get *results* who didn't *take action*. And while the results speak for themselves (my clients have added over $2.7 billion in sales as a result of coaching with me), none of it would have happened if they had sat around waiting for things to change.

Step 4: Do my Core 4 Formula that I teach you in this book on your top Afformations.

Step 5: Get support from me, your accountability partner, and/or one of my Power Habits® Certified Coaches until you get the results you desire. See the Recommended Resources at the back of this book for more information.

IF YOU WANT THINGS TO CHANGE, YOU'LL HAVE TO CHANGE THINGS.

WHAT THIS MEANS FOR YOU

Look, you want different results in your life, right? You want things to change, right? Well, that's the problem right there.

The problem is, we humans want *things* to change, but *we* don't want to change.

For example, in my keynote speeches, I often ask my audiences, "Who wants change?"

Every hand goes up.

Then I'll say, "Who wants to change?"

Crickets.

The obvious point is that we're all lunatics.

No, that's not the point. But it's not far wrong.

The fact is, anyone who wants to make more money, lose weight, find love, or be happy knows that they need to *take action* in order to get those results.

Yet, we humans are wired such that the last thing we want to do is change. Whether it's our behavior, our way of communicating with ourselves or others, or our thought process itself, like an old pair of slippers, we've gotten used to being comfortable—even if we're miserable!

That's why so many people would rather be *right* than rich.

So, ask yourself right now, "Would I rather be *right*, or would I rather be rich?"

If you'd rather be right (i.e., keep getting the results you're getting)—then just keep doing what you're doing. If, however, you'd rather be rich . . . then follow me.

SECTION II

THE MILLIONAIRE AFFORMATIONS®

- 5 -

HOW TO USE THE REST OF THIS BOOK

"A book should be luminous, not voluminous."

— Christian Nestell Bovee

This section of the book includes 301 of my favorite Millionaire Afformations. Of course, I could have written 1,001 or 10,001 Afformations. But I wanted this book to be shorter than *War and Peace*.

What's so magical about the number 301, you ask? In this book, you'll find seven chapters of my favorite Millionaire Afformations. I simply took the number 42—which is "the Answer to the Ultimate Question of Life, the Universe, and Everything," according to *The Hitchhiker's Guide to the Galaxy* by Douglas Adams—and added 1 to it, which gives us the number 43.

Why did I add 1 to 42? Since Mr. Adams never actually told us what the *question* was, and this book is all about *asking better questions,* I figured that I would simply +1 the answer in his honor.

Therefore, 7 X 43 = 301. Hence, the 301 Afformations in this book. (Wow, that may have been the longest and nerdiest explanation for anything I've ever done. You're welcome.)

I also highly recommend that you get the official *Millionaire Afformations Journal* so that you can write as many Millionaire Afformations as you like, in addition to the ones I've given you in this book. Order your own *Millionaire Afformations Journal* now at **www.MillionaireAfformations.com**.

GET THE OFFICIAL MILLIONAIRE AFFORMATIONS JOURNAL TO ACCELERATE YOUR RESULTS.

In order to accelerate your results even faster, you'll also want to do these three things:

1. **Get an AFFORMATIONS Study Buddy.** There are few things that will help you more than sharing this process with a like-minded individual. You can share your favorite Afformations and the subsequent results, as well as follow along in your *Millionaire Afformations Journal*.

For example, Babette and I do our Afformations together every day and marvel at all the amazing things that continue to happen in our lives (up to and including how this book came to be!).

2. **Start an AFFORMATIONS Book Study Group.** In addition to having an AFFORMATIONS Study Buddy, you'll also want to start an AFFORMATIONS Book Study Group. To start your own book study group, visit www.NoahStJohn.com/books.

3. **Check the boxes.** As you'll see in a moment, I've included checkboxes in front of all 301 Afformations so you can check off your favorite ones as you read through them. In addition, we've got space in the *Millionaire Afformations Journal* for you to write your own.

You can also refer to the Recommended Resources at the back of the book or visit **www.ShopNoahStJohn.com** to visit our online Success Store.

And now, enjoy your new Millionaire Afformations and start reaping new and better results in your life!

MEET MILLIONAIRE AFFORMER

JOHN CITO

I've been a fan of Dr. Noah St. John's work for over a decade. I first discovered Noah's work while I was going through a particularly challenging time in my life. Noah's methods helped me get through that time much faster and easier than I ever would have before.

In fact, Noah is the only thought leader I trust when it comes to helping me align my Inner Game and Outer Game.

When he announced his Millionaire AFFORMATIONS® Experiment, I was excited because I knew that Noah always provides tremendous value to his clients, customers, and students.

After completing just one day—one day!—of the Millionaire Afformations Experiment, I received notice that a client's six-figure account was finally being transferred to my wealth management company. Prior to that, I had been waiting for months without a word.

On Day 4, I received a call from a prospective client I hadn't spoken to in months. He told me that he and his wife wanted to move forward with my proposal. It resulted in a huge win for my firm.

In the process of doing the Experiment, I began to have a clearer picture of what action steps were necessary to make my Afformations a reality. As a result of reading, writing, speaking, and listening to my Afformations each day, I became more and more confident that I was on the right path and that opportunities would continue to present themselves. And they did!

In addition, ideas that would produce revenue started coming to me out of the blue. Once the ideas came, I wondered why I hadn't thought of them sooner. Then I realized that it was because I had been asking myself the wrong questions!

Thanks to Noah's methods, what was once murky and unclear has become simple, uncomplicated, and clear.

In addition, the more I use Afformations, the more my brain is compelled to answer them, which continues to produce feelings of confidence, self-worth, and happiness.

In short, this was a truly transformational experience, and I'm looking forward to what's to come as I continue to follow Noah St. John's life-changing methods!

- 6 -

AFFORMATIONS ON WEALTH

"The question isn't at what age I want to retire,
it's at what income."

— George Foreman

Whoever said, "Money doesn't buy happiness," clearly didn't know where to shop.

Seriously, if there's one area of life where many people are holding onto negative, disempowering beliefs, it's in the area of money, wealth, and abundance.

Why does this occur? Just look at some of the common things many of us were told about wealth (and rich people, in particular):

- Money doesn't grow on trees.
- Rich people are selfish.
- People get rich by taking advantage of others.
- If I have a lot of money, that means other people will have less.
- Rich people are greedy, money-obsessed, and miserly.
- Good people should not care about money.

Did you grow up hearing or believing any of these things? If so, know this: *Your relationship with money is like any other relationship you have.*

Imagine if you talked to your spouse the way you talk about money. *"You're bad; you're dirty, you're filthy, you're no good . . ."*

It's pretty easy to see that your spouse probably wouldn't be with you for very long if you treated them like that!

Imagine that money is a person. If you speak poorly about that person, they won't want to be with you. As strange as it may sound, money acts in the same way.

Now some people will disagree with the phrase, "Money acts." Some will say, "Noah, money doesn't *act* at all. Money is just a *thing* that sits there. It doesn't actually *do* anything."

To which I would say, "You're exactly right!"

It's true; money doesn't *do* anything. Each of us chooses to use money to do one thing or another. Money is simply a form of energy. In this way, money is like electricity; you can use it to light up your house, and you can use it to electrocute yourself. Electricity doesn't have a say in what you do with it, and neither does money.

TO ATTRACT MORE MONEY, CHANGE YOUR MONEY BELIEFS BY USING AFFORMATIONS.

Think about all the things you and I do every day related to money. Most of us work to get the thing called money. We drive to work to get the thing called money. We pay our bills so we can enjoy things like food, water, clothing, and shelter—all of which takes money. Even worrying about how we will pay our bills is thinking about money!

However, have you ever noticed that there is not one *positive* word in the English language to describe someone who "loves money"?

When we think of someone who loves money, we think of words like *miser, hoarder, selfish, greedy.* We might even picture Ebenezer Scrooge from *A Christmas Carol* (before the ghosts visited him and he had a change of heart, of course).

Yet, consider the following: If you speak ill of rich people, how are you ever going to be one of them?

Even Scrooge only became what most of us would consider "wealthy" when he began sharing his fortune with those less fortunate. Indeed, perhaps the only positive word for a person of wealth is *philanthropist*—yet even that word means that you must *give money away* to be seen positively.

I'm not suggesting that we should all become greedy, selfish people who hoard money. Nevertheless, the fact remains that you can do a lot more with money than without it.

For example, in my coaching practice, one way I help people is to take the guilt and shame out of being and wanting to be wealthy. That's one reason many of my clients make more in just twelve *weeks* of coaching with me than they made in the previous twelve *months*.

In fact, wealthy people do a ton of good in this world, from the people they employ directly to the people who are employed indirectly because of their businesses, purchases, and even their travel. From manufacturing to retail to the occasional meal out, having money means more money in motion. Focus on the positive things you can do with money, and see what miracles occur for you too.

Use the following *Millionaire Afformations on Wealth* to improve your relationship with money, so you can watch it become one of the most fulfilling relationships you'll ever have!

- ☐ Why am I so rich?
- ☐ Why am I so wealthy?
- ☐ Why do I always have enough money?
- ☐ Why is my credit so strong and healthy?
- ☐ Why is money no object?
- ☐ Why do I have enough money?
- ☐ Why do I have so much worth and value?
- ☐ Why does money come to me so easily?
- ☐ Why am I worth having a positive net worth?
- ☐ Why does my income always exceed my expenses?

- ☐ Why do I allow myself to be rich and happy too?
- ☐ Why is it okay for me to have lots of money?
- ☐ Why do I use my life of abundance to enrich the lives of others?
- ☐ Why do I enjoy finding new and creative ways to share my abundance?
- ☐ Why do I allow money to flow easily to me?
- ☐ Why am I so happy being so rich?
- ☐ Why does God bless me for the work I do?
- ☐ Why do my investments pay off so richly now that I seek sound advice?
- ☐ Why do I invest, tithe, and spend in balance?
- ☐ Why is money magnetized to me?
- ☐ Why do I give myself permission to be wealthy?
- ☐ Why does my health grow in proportion to my wealth?
- ☐ Why do I enjoy the benefits I bring to others through being abundant?
- ☐ Why can I be wealthy and spiritual at the same time?
- ☐ Why am I worth being wealthy?
- ☐ Why am I a money magnet?
- ☐ Why do I happily accept being wealthy?
- ☐ Why is it so easy to talk to my spouse about money?
- ☐ Why has God given me the power to obtain great wealth?
- ☐ Why is my credit being repaired?
- ☐ Why is money such a wonderful gift to me?
- ☐ Why do I teach my children the fine art of giving and receiving?
- ☐ Why do I trust that God always provides?
- ☐ Why do I thankfully ask and abundantly receive?
- ☐ Why is abundance attracted to me?
- ☐ Why does money love being with me?

☐ Why is it so easy to express my spirituality by being financially abundant?

☐ Why am I attracting money at this very moment?

☐ Why am I aligned with the energy of wealth and abundance?

☐ Why am I ready, willing, and able to receive more money?

☐ Why do I release all negative energy around money?

☐ Why can I handle massive success with ease and joy?

☐ Why do I love these Afformations on Wealth?

MEET MILLIONAIRE AFFORMER
LISA BROWNE

"If you let them into your house, you will never get it back."

You might be wondering how I got there. My husband and I were two payments behind in our "hard money" loan on our home. We thought that loan would be paid back in a short time. Life had other plans.

We got a phone call from a (supposedly) trusted real estate agent/ mortgage broker who convinced us to get the loan in the first place. Once we couldn't pay the exorbitant monthly payments, the same broker offered a solution. "Use my investor to rehab your house. Make it rentable to get income, and you can pay him back."

That sounded great, but their ultimate plan was to take control of the house.

When I explained my situation to a dear friend, she said, "Lisa, if you let them into your house, you will never get it back. They took your deed and recorded it in their name without your permission." That conversation happened in April 2021.

The broker and investor even tried to scare us with a three-day "pay or quit" demand. Then they sent us a thirty-day notice to move out.

My husband and I talked with everyone: realtors, friends, family, hard money lenders, mortgage brokers, loan brokers, and attorneys. They all said the same thing. No deed, no future.

You think the shutdown with the pandemic was bad? Try knowing that you would lose your house if you left it. After seven months of being prisoners in our home, I checked my email like I do every day and read Noah's message inviting me to his Experiment. I applied and got approval!

In only two weeks, I used Noah's Afformations to get through the final part of the most difficult time of my life. Things "magically" started shifting and changing. Options appeared as though orchestrated by outside forces. I blended Positive Prime with his Afformations and miracles (yes, miracles) seemed to appear.

People found ways to help us that could not have been possible in the past. Special people came into our lives who were strangers before—all in two weeks.

Those special people uncovered the fact that the threatening "deed" was false. The real estate broker and investor did not own the property at all.

During Noah's Afformations experiment, we worked with a notary public who happened to know a legitimate angel investor who had the means and desire to get the deed back for us.

The only stipulation with the new loan was that we walked away with a $2 million loan to be paid back in twelve months. Challenge accepted. We plan to repay the loan in six months because the interest rate is cut in half. The threat of foreclosure is gone!

At this time, February 28, 2022, the foreclosure is paid. Now we are free!

I want to personally thank Noah. These Afformations really work.

- 7 -

AFFORMATIONS
ON FOCUS

*"A major stimulant to creative thinking is focused questions.
There is something about a well-worded question
that often penetrates to the heart of the matter
and triggers new ideas and insights."*

— Brian Tracy

Why is the topic of *focus* in a book on becoming a millionaire, and why do so many people have so much trouble focusing?

Well, let's imagine that you want to reach a goal like . . . oh, I don't know . . . become a millionaire. (I took a guess.)

And let's say that you really, really want to reach that goal. Yet, for some reason, you never actually *do* anything about it.

Are you going to achieve your goal of becoming a millionaire? Unless you win the lottery or have a rich family member leave you a million dollars, I highly doubt it.

Notice that the question isn't whether you *deserve* to become a millionaire. Nor is it whether you were *lucky* enough to become a millionaire, nor whether you were born into the right family or the right neighborhood or got the right breaks in life.

The question is, what are you *doing* to reach your goal? And if you're not doing anything, why not?

This is where the question of *focus* comes in. Now some gurus say that FOCUS is an acronym for "Follow One Course Until Successful." I couldn't disagree more.

Take me as an example. When I was eighteen years old, I became a professional ballet dancer. My goal was to become the next Mikhail Baryshnikov.

Needless to say, I did not achieve that goal for several reasons—not the least of which was the fact that I had a career-ending injury at age twenty-two. That meant that at the age of twenty-two, I ended up with no job, no money, no connections, and no idea what to do with the rest of my life.

It's no surprise that less than three years later, after trying and failing at a number of different jobs, I decided to commit suicide. And although my life was spared at the last moment, I still had no idea what my purpose was or what to do with my life.

It wasn't until I discovered AFFORMATIONS in April 1997 that I finally knew what I wanted to do with the rest of my life. So, if I had followed the guru's advice and "Followed One Course Until Successful," I would probably be dead.

Now I'm certainly not suggesting that you should do all those crazy things that I did. However, I am encouraging you to realize that *focus* does not mean you should keep doing something you don't want to keep doing.

FOCUS DOESN'T ALWAYS MEAN "FOLLOW ONE COURSE UNTIL SUCCESSFUL."

To me, one of the most important aspects of focus is to eliminate distractions when you're working on a task, goal, or project.

For example, many people ask me, "Noah, how did you write all those books?"

My answer is: "By writing them."

Let me explain. Right now, at your fingertips, is a device that can bring you the entire accumulated knowledge of humanity. It can also bring you more than 149,000,000,000 videos on YouTube alone.

It can also enable you to watch sporting events from around the globe 24/7, from popular sports like football, baseball, and basketball to more obscure sports like cheese rolling, chess boxing, and extreme ironing (I swear I didn't make those up).

It can also allow you to play games like *Fortnite, Minecraft,* and *Hearthstone* to *Elastic Man, Teeth Runner,* and *Ear Clinic* (again, not making this up).

I think you know by now that I'm talking about your smartphone. What's ironic about that is that *smart*phones seem to be making us humans *dumber.*

That's why I refer to smartphones as Infinite Distraction Devices (IDDs). Because that's what they are—devices of infinite distraction. While smartphones have made our lives easier and more efficient in many ways, some experts say they have also created an entire generation of people who have been abducted by technology.

Many people think that focus is only a performance-based skill. However, it is much more than that.

FOCUS IS MUCH MORE THAN A PERFORMANCE-BASED SKILL.

For example, a person who can stay focused on a task will likely enjoy a high level of satisfaction. That, in turn, can lead to an improved quality of life. In addition, a person who can maintain high levels of focus can perform other tasks with far less effort.

The most important reason for having focused energy is to achieve your goals. If you're not able to stay focused, you won't accomplish much at all.

While distractions are inevitable, you need to decide which tasks are priorities and which are distractions. When you're not focused, you'll end up wasting hours doing trivial things. That's yet another reason why focus is a key factor in making progress toward your goal of becoming a millionaire (or any other goal, for that matter).

Therefore, use the following *Millionaire Afformations on Focus* to improve your focus so you can achieve your goals faster and easier than ever before!

- ☐ Why is it easy for me to focus on what I want to do?
- ☐ Why do I focus on my strengths and talents?
- ☐ Why do I focus on developing the skills that help me grow?
- ☐ Why do I bring my attention toward improving focus?
- ☐ Why is my focus growing stronger every day?
- ☐ Why is focus a natural part of me?
- ☐ Why do I focus on any task easily?
- ☐ Why is focusing becoming more effortless for me?
- ☐ Why do I choose to focus on all the good that happens in my life every day?
- ☐ Why do I focus on my blessings today?
- ☐ Why do I focus on my priorities before anything else?
- ☐ Why do I have more mental clarity now?
- ☐ Why do I love being alert and present?
- ☐ Why does being in the present make me feel alive and well?
- ☐ Why does doing my Afformations every day help me focus?
- ☐ Why do I ignore distractions and concentrate on the task at hand?
- ☐ Why do I remove all the thoughts and things in my life that don't serve me well?
- ☐ Why do I gain clarity as I put my intention toward what I want?
- ☐ Why do I realize my priorities?
- ☐ Why am I clear about what is most important in my life?
- ☐ Why am I clear about my priorities and values?
- ☐ Why am I able to make better decisions now that I'm more focused?
- ☐ Why do I know deep inside when to step forward and when to step back?
- ☐ Why do I let go of unnecessary arguments and needless debates?
- ☐ Why am I clear that my time and energy are precious and need to be invested in something purposeful every day?

☐ Why do I invest my time and energy wisely toward more meaningful things?

☐ Why do I give myself the gift of focus?

☐ Why do I choose to be a person of vision and value?

☐ Why is my life directed by my vision and priorities?

☐ Why am I able to focus more strongly with each passing day?

☐ Why am I in control of how I use my time?

☐ Why do I operate with the spirit of excellence?

☐ Why do I make good choices on a daily basis?

☐ Why am I so good at creating results?

☐ Why am I highly organized and mentally disciplined?

☐ Why am I in control of my thoughts, words, and actions?

☐ Why do I have a strong and disciplined mind?

☐ Why do I trust myself?

☐ Why am I capable enough to complete my tasks today?

☐ Why do I approach my goals with positivity, grit, and determination?

☐ Why do I get a lot done in a day?

☐ Why do I realize that *time* is the most precious resource I have?

☐ Why do I love these Afformations on Focus?

MEET MILLIONAIRE AFFORMER
DIANE EBLE

I have been doing Noah St. John's Afformations since reading his book *The Secret Code of Success*. I also took his Afformations course way back when it first came out. I use Afformations for everything: my health, my business, and my relationships. It even works on physical things, strangely enough. For instance, when I can't get my garage door to open with the keypad, I'll say an Afformation (Why is this working now?) and then it will.

Since I always do Afformations anyway, I wanted to participate in this experiment. I added a few Afformations from Noah to my regular ones and (most days) wrote them down, spoke them aloud, and listened as instructed.

Since I see miracles all the time through Afformations, I tried to pay special attention to the things that changed in terms of my wealth. What I needed to work on most was the work-life balance and receiving wealth.

What I noticed was that money came in unexpectedly.

For instance, a couple of people I had made affiliate sales with paid me. One was from a year ago! There was a glitch in her program, which she fixed. It took a whole year to get it, and it didn't happen until I had done Afformations. (I think I was using something about being a money magnet.)

Also, an unexpected opportunity came up to promote products I believe in. There was no affiliate program before, but now that appears to be in place. I was feeling blocked about starting a project—a whole new direction, really—in my business, and now I'm forging ahead.

Right after I finished the Afformations Experiment, I went on a business retreat for three days. It was fantastic, and I emerged with very clear direction and confidence about the new direction for my business.

Also, for the past fifteen months, I have been embroiled in trying to settle my mother's estate in the context of a very complicated, dysfunctional family. My co-executor has been pressuring me to take on the financial responsibility of herself and two of my brothers, and I have been refusing. In the past couple of weeks, I have been able to stand strong in the face of all her manipulative tactics.

So, these are the things I noticed since doing the Millionaire Afformations Experiment. As I said, I love Afformations and will use them for the rest of my life. I also teach them to my coaching clients and encourage them to explore Noah's work. I have been following Noah since the early *Permission to Succeed* days, and I think his work is brilliant!

- 8 -

AFFORMATIONS ON SELF-CONFIDENCE

"When you act, act effortlessly, as if you could do much more. Avoid the temptation of revealing how hard you work— it only raises questions."

— Robert Greene

To say that self-confidence is important to becoming a millionaire is like saying that if a blue whale were laid longways on a basketball court, the game would be canceled.

In other words . . . *Duh!*

High levels of self-confidence are crucial to being successful in life. That's because people who are confident in themselves are more likely to:

✓ Set healthy boundaries

✓ Speak up against unfairness

✓ Be more successful in their careers

✓ Feel more comfortable meeting new people

✓ Believe in themselves enough to pursue their dreams

✓ Have the inner strength to take risks

✓ Listen to the opinions of others without being defensive

✓ Take the actions necessary to achieve their goals

Moreover, a lack of self-confidence is one of the most common reasons people make poor decisions. People who lack self-confidence often rely on other people to make decisions for them, which can lead straight to making bad decisions.

Believe me, I speak from personal experience. I've already told you that when I launched SuccessClinic.com in 1997 in that 300-square-foot basement apartment, I had no money, no connections, no marketing skills, no sales experience, and no business acumen.

What I didn't mention was that I also had *zero* self-confidence. Now, that may sound counterintuitive, because I also told you that I knew I would never give up until I reached my goals.

But the fact is because I didn't believe in myself, I allowed other people to push me around and take advantage of me. And that cost me, big time.

> **WITHOUT SELF-CONFIDENCE, YOU'LL MISS OUT ON A LOT OF OPPORTUNITIES.**

Case in point: When my first book, *Permission to Succeed*®, was published in 1999, I was contacted by a man named Chris Byrne, who goes by the moniker, "The Toy Guy."

He told me that he absolutely loved my book and that it changed his life. He also told me he had been on *The Oprah Winfrey Show* and that he was going to recommend my book to one of the senior producers on the show.

Of course, having Oprah endorse your book is the dream of every author with a pulse. My dream was coming true—and it happened all by itself! It seemed too good to be true.

Sadly, what happened next is one of the greatest regrets of my life. Because I still didn't believe in myself at the time, I ended up hiring a "publicist" to help me get on *The Oprah Winfrey Show*. (I put that word in quotation marks because her only qualification was that she called herself a publicist.)

Now you might say, "But Noah, why would you hire a publicist when you were already referred to the senior producer at *The Oprah Winfrey Show?*"

Exactly.

Because I didn't believe in myself. Because I had no self-confidence. Because I didn't think I could do it.

And because that "publicist" had no idea what she was doing, I ended up losing that opportunity of a lifetime, and I never did get to appear on *The Oprah Winfrey Show*.

Let that be a lesson to you. When life hands you a golden opportunity, don't go asking people who have no idea what they're doing to tell you what to do or stop you from doing what *you* have to do.

For example, many times in my life I've had no idea what I was supposed to do next. Even worse, for the first ten years after I launched SuccessClinic.com, even though I was helping people around the world to believe in themselves, I still didn't believe in myself.

That's one reason why it took much longer than it should have to reach my goals. The raw, unfiltered truth is that I lacked the self-confidence I was instilling in others.

People with self-confidence are more likely to make positive changes when things don't go as planned. They're more likely to push past barriers and achieve their big goals. That level of self-assurance will allow you to share your talents and opinions, and it will help you reach your full potential.

That's why having self-confidence is one of the most important keys to abundant living and becoming a millionaire. When you have self-confidence, you have no reason to fear failure.

HAVING SELF-CONFIDENCE ALLOWS YOU TO COME BACK AFTER A SETBACK.

It's about knowing your worth and trusting your ability to do the right thing. You'll know that you're capable of overcoming obstacles and achieving your goals.

And when you're confident, you don't care if you fail—because you'll keep trying until you do find the right path.

In short, developing your self-confidence is essential in every area of your life because being confident means empowering yourself and others.

It means you are more likely to reach out to others and notice when they are suffering.

When you're confident in yourself, you'll be able to look in the mirror and admire yourself without fear.

Therefore, use the following *Millionaire Afformations on Self-Confidence* to boost your confidence so you can celebrate your strengths, embrace your weaknesses, and be all the happier for it!

- ☐ Why am I stronger than I know?
- ☐ Why do I find the positive in any situation?
- ☐ Why can I handle whatever the day has in store?
- ☐ Why is today going to be a great day?
- ☐ Why am I great at setting healthy boundaries?
- ☐ Why do I love my body?
- ☐ Why do I have the ability to dream as big and as far as I want?
- ☐ Why do I know it's okay to take care of myself?
- ☐ Why do I know it's healthy to take personal time for myself and my mental health?
- ☐ Why am I responsible, capable, and motivated?
- ☐ Why am I worthy of love and happiness?
- ☐ Why am I happy to be alive and to be myself?
- ☐ Why do I get to live life to the fullest?
- ☐ Why do I build supportive and healthy relationships?
- ☐ Why am I enthusiastic and full of energy?
- ☐ Why am I so good at finding the best in others and in myself too?
- ☐ Why are my experiences and the lessons I've learned important and valuable?
- ☐ Why do I enjoy working toward my goals?
- ☐ Why do I have a deep respect for myself?
- ☐ Why does my work bring me enjoyment and help me become the person I want to be?

☐ Why is my self-confidence growing every day?

☐ Why is it true that no one and nothing can hold me back?

☐ Why do I feel joy and peace in this very moment?

☐ Why am I ready for anything?

☐ Why am I surrounded by loving and supportive people?

☐ Why am I strong and smart enough to make it through this challenge and learn from it?

☐ Why do I deserve good things, just like anyone else?

☐ Why do I deeply and completely love and accept myself now?

☐ Why am I easy to love?

☐ Why do I deserve to be happy too?

☐ Why do I radiate self-love and confidence?

☐ Why am I worthy and deserving of love?

☐ Why am I peaceful, happy, healthy, and free to be me?

☐ Why am I safe to be who I really am?

☐ Why do I choose to be kind to myself today?

☐ Why is *now* my time to shine?

☐ Why do I get to live the life of my dreams?

☐ Why do I believe in the person I am becoming?

☐ Why am I always enough?

☐ Why am I exactly who I need to be in this moment?

☐ Why am I worthy of love, peace, and joy?

☐ Why do I love who I am in this moment?

☐ Why do I love these Afformations on Self-Confidence?

MEET MILLIONAIRE AFFORMER
ERICA LATRICE

Prior to Millionaire Afformations, I had been introduced to Afformations and encouraged my fourteen-year-old daughter to start using them. One area, in particular, was for basketball—a sport she had only played for a few months. One of her statements was that she would be a starter on varsity as a freshman. It seemed impossible based on her experience. When she was suddenly moved up to varsity and announced as a starter, we were ecstatic!

My main thought was, *I must get back to doing these!* Less than twenty-four hours after that, the Millionaire Afformations Experiment came my way!

Since starting, in less than two weeks, I added $8,000 of income and counting. I am down ten pounds after a few weeks, which I can only guess is a product of being more focused. On average, I have been waking up almost two hours earlier than usual, and the results have been a game-changer for my business.

My prayer time has been much deeper now that I feel way more focused—not to mention the ideas and opportunities that have come my way.

I appreciate Noah's genuineness in every work he has written. As a reader, I know how it feels to wonder if this is just happening for everyone else but not realistic for me. However, it works! Thank you so much for Millionaire Afformations. I know that this is just the beginning.

- 9 -

AFFORMATIONS ON GOAL SETTING AND GOAL ACHIEVEMENT

*"The question I ask myself like almost every day is,
'Am I doing the most important thing I could be doing?'"*

— Mark Zuckerberg

If you want to be rich, you must set goals. By creating a list of your desires, you will become more motivated to achieve them. You can also write down your ideas and goals whenever and wherever you have them.

Sometimes, the best ideas come to you when you take a break from work. Make sure you write them down so you can remember them later. It is very likely that you'll have to update your goals once you hit them—but remember to celebrate every success!

That's another lesson that took me a long time to learn. When I was growing up, my father was a very hard worker (he still is!) who never took the time to celebrate his wins.

For example, when I was five years old, he moved our family to Kennebunkport, Maine to pursue his dream of being in the theater.

Even though he didn't have much money at the time, he decided that he would build us a house because he said (and this is a direct quote), "How hard can it be?"

Because our family had very little money, my father put my brother and me to work helping him build the house. Now, when you're five years old, there's not much you can do to help build a house except mix cement and hold things. So that's exactly what I did.

The funny thing is, with my father, there was no such thing as "taking breaks." He would work from before sunrise to after sunset, frequently without so much as a lunch break. Naturally, my brother and I had to adhere to the same punishing work schedule. Back then, we simply didn't know any better.

The point of the story is that I never learned how to stop and celebrate my wins. I thought the point of life was to work and work and work and work and work and work . . . until one day, you drop dead at your desk. (Who knows? Perhaps that is how I'll go.)

However, I learned the hard way that if all you do is work, work, work . . . sooner or later, the work itself becomes very unsatisfying.

ALL WORK AND NO PLAY SUCKS.

That's why, to achieve your goals, you need to make them attainable and measurable. Whether you want to increase your impact, influence, or income (or all of the above), you need to create a list of short-term and long-term goals so you can measure your progress and celebrate your wins.

In addition to having goals, millionaires have the vision, plans, and flexibility to make changes along the way. Having a clear picture of what you want is the best way to create your vision. Using a clear vision and having a clear plan will make your dreams a reality. That is why goal setting is so crucial to becoming a millionaire.

Aside from setting goals, you should also set a clear timeline to achieve them. Achieving your goals will help you stay motivated to work on your vision. Moreover, a good plan will help you set the right mindset to accomplish your objectives. In general, if you have a positive mindset and a strong desire, you will be able to achieve success in life.

You should set goals that are specific and measurable. It's best to aim high—aim for what you might think is impossible. But remember to be realistic, too. As I've shown you in this book, most people make subconscious decisions based on their emotional state.

In addition, having a goal that's too general (like "Make a lot of money") will only make it more difficult for you to achieve it. It's better to set a specific goal (like "Make XXX dollars by XXX date") and then work toward it.

In addition to your personal and professional goals, you should also have a team to help you achieve your goal. By building a team, you'll be more likely to succeed.

Remember to set realistic goals for your team, as well. That will help them work toward their individual dreams as well as the team goals. However, if the goals are either too vague or too easy to reach, they'll likely lose focus and motivation.

When you set goals that inspire you, motivate you, and even scare you a little, you're well on your way to becoming the rich, happy person you want to be.

Therefore, use the following *Millionaire Afformations on Goal Setting and Goal Achievement* so you can accelerate your progress faster than you ever thought possible!

- ☐ Why am I capable of achieving my goals?
- ☐ Why do I allow love to guide me in all the actions I take?
- ☐ Why is my mind open to new possibilities?
- ☐ Why do I look for positivity in every situation?
- ☐ Why do I have what I need to reach my goals?
- ☐ Why can I handle anything that's in my way?
- ☐ Why do I have enormous courage within me all the time?
- ☐ Why do I have the determination to keep moving ahead in life?
- ☐ Why do I have the persistence to pursue my dreams?
- ☐ Why are my goals more important than any fear that might hold me back?
- ☐ Why am I stronger than my fears?

- ☐ Why do I create magic in whatever I do?
- ☐ Why can I create the life that I dream of?
- ☐ Why am I in control of whatever I wish to do with my life?
- ☐ Why do my present circumstances *not* dictate my future?
- ☐ Why is my reality determined by my positive energy?
- ☐ Why will I manifest anything I focus on?
- ☐ Why do I cherish the life I am creating every day?
- ☐ Why do I seize every opportunity that flows to me?
- ☐ Why do I always choose to lead by my heart and the path it makes for my goals?
- ☐ Why are my goals guided by the desires of my heart?
- ☐ Why am I living a life that is aligned with my highest truth?
- ☐ Why do I have immense faith in myself and seek the truth within me?
- ☐ Why is abundant wealth and prosperity coming to me now?
- ☐ Why do I attract positivity and abundance?
- ☐ Why am I worthy of dreaming big?
- ☐ Why am I grateful for what I already have while I keep striving to get what I really want?
- ☐ Why am I motivated and ready to take any action that pulls me closer to achieving my goals?
- ☐ Why am I open to seeking help from people who are more knowledgeable and can facilitate my dreams?
- ☐ Why do I devote my time to planning, researching, and *taking action* to achieve my goals?
- ☐ Why do I build a strong network of people who help me reach my goals faster and easier than I would by working alone?
- ☐ Why do I improve my communication skills every day?
- ☐ Why do I only associate with positive and supportive people who encourage me and my dreams?

☐ Why do I have the power to unlock my full potential?

☐ Why did I reach my most audacious goals faster than I ever thought possible?

☐ Why do I come up with creative ideas that help advance my goals?

☐ Why am I a proactive human being?

☐ Why did I stop procrastinating and choose to act in the present to make my future better?

☐ Why do I believe in taking daily positive *action* instead of just talking about my goals?

☐ Why do I keep track of my time and understand its importance?

☐ Why do I start my projects early and finish on time?

☐ Why am I aiming toward higher goals every day and striving to achieve them before each day ends?

☐ Why do I love these Afformations on Goal Setting and Goal Achievement?

MEET MILLIONAIRE AFFORMER

KATHERINE HERRERA

My name is Katherine, and I'm from Costa Rica. This Challenge came to me at a very important moment of my life. When I subscribed to the Experiment, I was happy to use the Afformations to increase my income and have better results with my business. I really needed to get economic stability, and I was feeling that something with my business was not working because, for a long time, I was unable to get the results I expected. I am a psychologist, and I also have a cardboard box factory.

I was very hopeful with my participation in the Experiment, and I was focused on the impact it was going to make on my relationship with money. However, three days before we started, I used my credit card to go to the doctor because I had some symptoms. He discovered something in my body that required a very expensive surgery. First, I was a little sad and scared, but then I decided to include in my Experiment an Afformation related to health.

Since the first day, I was feeling hopeful and enjoyed the time I took for my Afformations. A new client called me that day because he was interested in my psychological service. I noticed that my Afformation about attracting the correct people at the correct time was starting to bring changes to my life.

On the second day, my phone was ringing a lot. Many different clients called to get information about my cardboard products, and I also got to find an office I needed to work with my clients near home.

Over the next few days, I received money from my business and was able to pay some bills in advance, so I was feeling better about the way I was in control of my money. I also received $200 from a very good friend; she wanted to contribute to the medical expenses I charged some days ago on my credit card.

New things happened every day while I was using my Afformations for the Experiment. My business had more activity, and I also found two excellent clients who not only bought some of my products but also needed to continue buying these products every week. Stability—exactly what I was looking for!

Lots of more beautiful things happened. I received calls from very good friends with great news on their lives; I improved my relationship with people I love and had beautiful moments with them, I received excellent feedback from my psychological patients, and they told me about how the therapy has brought positive changes in their lives.

Now, I can really feel that I am attracting abundance to my life at every moment, but it is not only about money, but also, I can feel a very good life balance.

Afformations brought magic to my life. Now, better clients come to me frequently, my relationships are much better, and my physical symptoms have completely disappeared.

- 10 -

AFFORMATIONS ON PURPOSE

"Sometimes a particular purpose can be squared with a particular career. It may take nothing more than reexamining your career, asking some questions, and discovering a purpose you have overlooked in the past."

— Vince Lombardi

Knowing your purpose is one of the most important factors to becoming wealthy, because millionaires know there is more to life than just a paycheck.

Wealthy people understand that they must have a higher purpose in order to succeed. That's why millionaires don't simply set goals; they also have a clear *purpose* and *vision* for their lives.

A truly wealthy person is one who makes a difference in the lives of others. That mindset often requires a leap of faith because many people don't know how they can make a difference in the lives of others.

Whether you're just getting started or have been at this for a while, start building a team of people who will help you achieve your goals and realize your purpose. This is crucial because it will drive you to reach your goals and add value to the lives of others.

Also, whether you're working toward becoming a millionaire, multi-millionaire, or billionaire, it's essential to have a compelling vision and a clear plan of action for the future. That often means you must take that leap of faith and start building your team before you feel like you're ready.

A millionaire's daily and weekly routines set them up for success. They create a system for making critical decisions and are disciplined in sticking to it. Achieving your goals is not luck; you must prepare for it.

That's why the best way to become a millionaire is to begin to think like a millionaire right now. However, that does not mean you have to go out and start spending a lot of money on needless things. In fact, you need to pick the right people and opportunities to invest in.

Nevertheless, by being generous, you can help yourself while also helping others. That's why a millionaire's life is filled with people, purpose, and passion.

> **MILLIONAIRES INVEST IN THE RIGHT PEOPLE AND THE RIGHT OPPORTUNITIES.**

A millionaire's purpose is to give and receive in balance. The irony is that many people have very strong giving muscles but very weak receiving muscles.

What is the purpose of life? That is for each one of us to decide. However, when you build a network of supportive people and create a positive impact in the world, your life will be far more meaningful. You'll feel more content and satisfied with your work. Whether you're working or helping others, you'll have a better sense of direction and a better understanding of what's truly important to you.

In the case of an entrepreneur, that means finding ways to use your unique strengths and overcome challenges. The most successful people are those willing to learn from their experiences and adapt to change. By doing that, you will increase your chances of success and make your life, and the lives of those around you, far better.

Therefore, use the following *Millionaire Afformations on Purpose* so you can embody your vision and make your dreams a reality!

☐ Why do I wake up every morning with a strong connection to my life purpose?

☐ Why do I stay true to myself?

☐ Why am I conscious of my time and my life?

☐ Why do I matter?

☐ Why am I fearless in the pursuit of my life purpose?

☐ Why is my life purpose waiting for me with open arms?

☐ Why do I have something special to offer this world?

☐ Why are my talents needed?

☐ Why am I just as important as anyone else?

☐ Why does what I do with my life matter?

☐ Why is my life purpose becoming more and more clear to me every day?

☐ Why am I grateful for the divine guidance and inspiration I'm receiving now?

☐ Why do I receive divine guidance with gratitude?

☐ Why am I open to trying new things?

☐ Why am I meant to live a life of meaning, purpose, joy, and fulfillment?

☐ Why do I have the energy and resources I need to pursue and fulfill my higher purpose?

☐ Why am I capable of achieving anything I set my mind to?

☐ Why do I trust my inner voice and intuition?

☐ Why do I honor my truth?

☐ Why do I have the power to create a deeply meaningful and purposeful life for myself?

☐ Why am I brave and committed to the fulfillment of my higher purpose?

☐ Why am I motivated to achieve my life purpose?

☐ Why can I do whatever I set my mind to?

☐ Why do I walk confidently in the direction of my life purpose?

☐ Why do I take steps every day to fulfill my life purpose?

☐ Why do I deserve to live a life of passion, magic, and miracles?

☐ Why do I release perfectionism?

☐ Why do I know what my life purpose is?

☐ Why am I attuned to the callings and longings of my soul?

☐ Why am I walking in alignment with my higher purpose every day?

☐ Why am I succeeding in my life purpose?

☐ Why do I succeed by attracting the right people who help me fulfill my life purpose?

☐ Why am I full of vitality, zest, and joy?

☐ Why am I happy with who I am?

☐ Why am I capable of living my life purpose?

☐ Why do I attract the right people at the right time?

☐ Why do I let go of old, negative beliefs that no longer serve me?

☐ Why am I now open to limitless possibilities?

☐ Why am I capable of attracting abundance every day?

☐ Why do my actions create constant wealth, prosperity, and abundance for me and those I love?

☐ Why am I worthy enough to follow my dreams and manifest my desires?

☐ Why do I choose to embrace my life purpose today?

☐ Why do I love these Afformations on Purpose?

MEET MILLIONAIRE AFFORMER
DIXIE HICKMAN

I signed up for the Millionaire Mindset Experiment for two reasons:

1. I believe in Noah St. John's formula for adjusting your mindset into more productive patterns.
2. I wasn't doing it, and I needed an external push to apply it.

The hardest part was getting a rhythm for the Core 4 Formula each morning. Reading selected Afformations for a minute was easy, as was writing out some of my favorites. Choosing one for the Afformation of the Day to be recited for a minute provoked a bit of creative fun. Listening was the challenging part, requiring headphones and a recording. Noah's one-minute stress buster was a favorite fall-back or a section of his Health recording. I look forward to figuring out how to record my own voice and favorite Afformations.

By the end of the second week, the habit pattern was in place, and I found myself *afforming* to myself throughout the day. This fortunate development served me well when an illness flattened me for three days—no writing, no reading, no listening. But I kept *afforming*. "Why do I heal so quickly and easily?" "Why am I a magnet for money and health?" Every time I caught myself feeling down, I countered with, "Why am I in control of my thoughts and actions?" "Why do I choose thoughts from my deep store of cheerful and loving thoughts?"

Day 12 presented me with a refund for an overpayment on a loan—$401.27, a delightfully unexpected surprise! Day 20 brought a $50,000 check from a departed cousin's estate, an expected gift but delivered way ahead of schedule.

Why do I keep this habit of the Core 4 fresh in my life?

- 11 -

AFFORMATIONS ON WORK-LIFE BALANCE

"The challenge of work-life balance is without question one of the most significant struggles faced by modern man."

— Stephen Covey

Time is the most valuable resource we have. While money and energy are also valuable, both can be replaced. Time, however, once spent, can never be replaced.

That's why highly successful people make sure they balance their time between work and life. They make the time to operate successful businesses or have great careers while also spending time with their families and doing things that light the spark within them.

To create a healthy work-life balance, you need to find work that you love and enjoy devoting a healthy amount of time to while also devoting time to things outside of work that bring you joy.

Sure, it might take some time to get there, but the result will be well worth it. If you do, you'll be on the road to financial freedom. That isn't something that can be done overnight, but it's a goal you'll have for the rest of your life.

When starting a business or venture, you often must put in long hours. For example, when I started SuccessClinic.com in 1997, since I had no idea how to run a successful online business, I worked fourteen to eighteen hours a day, seven days a week.

However, that kind of punishing schedule isn't something you should be doing forever. In fact, one of your main focuses should be to install the right Systems of Support as soon as possible, so you don't have to work all those crazy hours.

The point of work is to support your life, not the other way around. If you own a business, that business should exist to support the lifestyle you desire. But far too many entrepreneurs and business owners feel like their business is running *them*.

I'VE HELPED MANY PEOPLE DISCOVER HOW TO BALANCE WORK AND LIFE.

It's essential to take time off for yourself. Your career should be secondary to your health and well-being. By setting priorities, you'll have a better chance of success in your personal and professional life.

If you can't find balance between your personal and professional life, you should consider seeking help from a business coach or mentor so you can begin to remove yourself from the business while still making more money than before.

Over the last twenty-five years of coaching Hollywood celebrities, seven- and eight-figure CEOs, professional athletes, and elite entrepreneurs, I've helped many hard-driving people to stop feeling guilty for taking time off work. But it's not as easy as it sounds.

If you feel guilty taking time off work, that's all the more reason to hire a coach to help you install the right systems to help you succeed.

It's impossible to be successful or happy if you are not living the life you've chosen for yourself. That's because you need to live your life in harmony with your priorities, values, and deepest desires. When you're living a life that combines all of the above, you've got the recipe for long-lasting success and fulfillment.

Use the following *Millionaire Afformations on Work-Life Balance* so you can enjoy a better balance of work and life!

☐ Why do I love my life?

☐ Why do I love my work?

☐ Why do I have a wonderful work-life balance?

☐ Why do I balance my work and life now?

☐ Why do I make time to relax?

☐ Why am I so productive at work?

☐ Why do I make time for my friends and family?

☐ Why do I have faith in myself?

☐ Why do I easily manage all aspects of my life and work?

☐ Why do I enjoy my balanced life?

☐ Why do I make sure that I give quality time to my family?

☐ Why do I balance my work and life effortlessly?

☐ Why do I say *no* when it serves my larger purpose?

☐ Why do I say *yes* to things that serve my highest good?

☐ Why do I give my equal contribution to both work and life?

☐ Why do I pay equal attention to both work and life?

☐ Why do I take regular breaks from work?

☐ Why am I fully present when I am with family and friends outside of work?

☐ Why do I enjoy the perfect balance of work, play, and rest?

☐ Why do I arrange my physical, emotional, spiritual, and professional lives perfectly?

☐ Why do I let go of work pressure?

☐ Why do I let go of mental stress?

☐ Why do I keep my work at my workplace?

☐ Why do I keep my family issues at home?

☐ Why do I know how to balance work and life?

☐ Why am I making my life harmonious?

☐ Why do I have the work and not let the work have me anymore?

☐ Why do I make time for work and time for me as well?

☐ Why am I more capable of balancing my work and life every day?

☐ Why do I forgive myself and others?

☐ Why is everything working out for my highest good?

☐ Why do I say yes to life and life says yes to me?

☐ Why are all areas of my life harmonious and balanced?

☐ Why do I make the time to work on my most important goals every day?

☐ Why do I achieve a greater balance between my thoughts and actions every day?

☐ Why is every area of my life in perfect balance now?

☐ Why are my life goals in perfect balance?

☐ Why are all aspects of my life in perfect alignment?

☐ Why am I creating my ideal future with every thought?

☐ Why do I choose to let go of hurt and resentment now?

☐ Why do I set myself free?

☐ Why am I divinely guided and always protected?

☐ Why do I love these Afformations on Work-Life Balance?

MEET MILLIONAIRE AFFORMER
MICHAEL QUAST

So . . . when I received the email for the 14-day, 5-minute-a-day "challenge" to create a millionaire mindset, I thought, *five minutes a day laid out with an easy step-by-step plan? Heck yeah! I can do that.* I love personal development, and my mind was open to a possibility.

I've recited many affirmations over and over through the years. I was really never sure if they were making any headway or traction or helping in any way. It felt like I was forcing it—trying to convince myself I was rich . . . or 180 pounds of lean muscle. Or whatever the affirmation of the week was. Results were short-lived at best.

I met Noah many years ago at a seminar, and his principle of asking questions to yourself and the practice of Afformation always made sense to me. Ask a question of your mind and it goes to work to find the answer. Seemed pretty simple, so I decided to answer the email and join the challenge.

Read, write, speak, and listen five minutes a day to Afformations of my choice (a huge list was provided). I started as soon as I got the Challenge guide in my inbox. There was a certain feeling that I got from the process. It just felt good.

I feel energy flowing. Not sure of the explanation behind it, but the fourteen days have yielded some pretty cool results. December and January, prior to beginning, I felt as if I was running in mud—couldn't get out of my own way. Literally, the day after I started, I got two checks in the mail. Not huge, but both were pretty random and unexpected—totaling about $150. In the following two weeks, I wrote two real estate contracts and closed another deal. My lead flow has picked up, and I am in the process of listing two to four more properties and working with several qualified, motivated buyers, none of which were in process before the challenge . . . in two weeks!

I have continued the 5-minute daily Afformation practice because I truly enjoy it. I try to do it in the morning, though I'm not always perfect with it. If I run out early and I'm in my truck, I will put on some recordings of Afformations that I made and listen while driving. It sets my energy heading in a positive trajectory for the day and helps me feel powerful. The outcomes are evident. I am excited to see how continuing to Afform will compound my results moving forward.

Stay tuned!

Thank you, Noah, for this gift.

AFFORMATIONS ON MILLIONAIRE HABITS

*"I had a clear vision of myself winning the Mr. Universe contest.
It was a very spiritual thing, in a way, because I had such faith
in the route, the path, that there was never a question in my
mind that I would make it."*

— Arnold Schwarzenegger

Millionaires follow certain specific habits that make it possible to become wealthy, happy, and fulfilled. For example, in my online course **Power Habits® Academy**, I teach you how to admit what you truly desire, identify exactly what's stopping you from having it, and give yourself permission to live a joyfully happy, fulfilling and rich life.

That might sound like a mouthful, but the essential truth is that most highly successful people became that way by following a system of unconscious habits that enabled them to become wealthy, happy, and fulfilled.

The irony is that every one of these habits is *the exact opposite* of what the gurus teach! That's one reason so many people hire me after they've reached a certain level of success, only to discover that the old ways don't allow them to advance any further.

You can learn more about 7-Figure Life Academy at **www.7FigureLifeAcademy.com** as well as our other coaching programs at **www.ShopNoahStJohn.com**.

In addition, here are some of the most important habits you can do to become a millionaire:

1. Read. The old saying is true: "Leaders are readers." However, because time is the most valuable resource we have, what kind of books should you spend your time reading?

I recommend reading two different kinds of books each month—one for education and one for entertainment. Remember when I talked about work-life balance in the previous chapter—the fact is, you should make reading for entertainment and pleasure just as important as reading to advance your career.

2. Track your money. I love spreadsheets. (Nerd alert!) If you don't know where your money is going every month, pretty soon, it will be gone, and you won't know what hit you.

Track your income and spending on a spreadsheet because this will enable you to see trends over time and adapt accordingly.

> **STOP TRYING TO IMPRESS OTHER PEOPLE WITH ALL THE STUFF YOU HAVE.**

3. Live below your means. The image many of us have about being a millionaire is lavish spending on yachts, planes, and cars. While there certainly are millionaires who do that, it's more accurate to say that most millionaires live pretty . . . well, let's just say it . . . boring lives.

My favorite book on this subject is *The Millionaire Next Door* by Thomas J. Stanley and William D. Danko. The authors show through scientific research why most millionaires live average lifestyles, while many people who try to *look like they're rich* are typically not doing well financially.

My favorite phrase from the book is, "Big hat, no cattle," which refers to someone with lots of showy objects but no real net worth (or, indeed, is deep in debt).

Bottom line: To be a millionaire, stop trying to impress people with all the fancy stuff you buy. Instead, focus on being a person of true wealth and positive net worth, because that will lead to being financially free rather than chained to your *stuff*.

4. Choose the right people. It's true that we tend to become the average of the five people we spend the most time with. That's why it's crucial to choose the right people to surround yourself with while also removing the people who do not support your dreams and vision.

5. Install the right systems. Installing the right Systems of Support is a crucial habit for becoming a millionaire. The five essential Systems of Support are: People, Activities, Environment, Introspection, and Simplify. You can discover how I help my clients install these Systems of Support at **www.FreeGiftfromNoah.com**.

6. Be physically active. There's an old saying, "The person who has their health has many problems, but the person who doesn't have their health has only one problem." It's clear that millions of people don't eat right or get enough exercise. What good is having lots of money if you don't have the health to enjoy it?

Be sure to stay physically active throughout your lifetime and eat the right foods to treat your body as the temple it is. Last time I checked, we only get one body on this trip called *life*, so be nice to the one you've got.

7. Cultivate a positive attitude. The millionaire lifestyle involves a consistent practice of self-motivation, discipline, and positivity. The single best thing you can do to cultivate this habit is to use Afformations!

Use the following *Millionaire Afformations on Habits* so you can achieve greater success, happiness, and fulfillment in your life and your career!

☐ Why do I have millionaire habits?

☐ Why do my habits support my new, rich lifestyle?

☐ Why do I practice better habits so I can live an abundant life?

☐ Why do I deserve to be rich, happy, and fulfilled?

☐ Why do my actions lead to abundance and prosperity for myself and my family?

☐ Why am I living in limitless abundance?

☐ Why am I thankful for the abundance and prosperity in my life?

☐ Why do I open my heart to accept all the abundance the Universe has for me?

☐ Why does my cup overflow with prosperity?

☐ Why do my actions create constant wealth?

☐ Why do I deserve to be abundant?

☐ Why are positive people drawn to me?

☐ Why am I open to receiving limitless abundance?

☐ Why do I have whatever I need to succeed?

☐ Why do opportunities continue to come to me?

☐ Why are all doors to prosperity open to me?

☐ Why do I attract endless abundance through living in gratitude?

☐ Why does everything I touch turn to gold?

☐ Why do I embrace new avenues of income?

☐ Why do I control my money and not allow money to control me?

☐ Why am I grateful for the financial security that is constant in my life?

☐ Why am I becoming richer and happier every day?

☐ Why do I share my riches with joy?

☐ Why do I make money doing what I love?

☐ Why am I open to all the wealth life has for me?

☐ Why do I release all negative energy about money?

☐ Why do I spend my money wisely?

☐ Why do I get to be financially free?

☐ Why do I give myself permission to release toxic thoughts?

☐ Why is my body empowered with increased energy every day?

☐ Why do I radiate positivity?

☐ Why am I capable of achieving my dreams?

☐ Why do I have the ability to create absolutely anything I want?

☐ Why are my dreams coming true now?

☐ Why do I grow stronger and more capable of manifesting my dreams every day?

☐ Why do I have everything I need to create anything I desire?

☐ Why am I attracting the right people, resources, and capital to support all my goals?

☐ Why do I consistently take any needed actions to increase my wealth?

☐ Why do I have the capacity to change the lives of people around the world?

☐ Why am I creating opportunities that benefit people all over the world?

☐ Why do I consistently attract other millionaires to network with and learn from?

☐ Why do I let nothing stop me from reaching my goals and fulfilling my mission and vision?

☐ Why do I love these Afformations on Millionaire Habits?

MEET MILLIONAIRE AFFORMER

DR. KENYATTA JONES

I was so excited to be a part of your experiment. Although I started on February 3, I did complete the entire 14-day challenge. On Day 1, I finally got a resolution to an issue with AT&T, which had lingered on for six months. The free phone (a $700+ value) I received is better than what they initially promised me in July.

On Day 2, the publicist of a businessman/attorney reached out to me. I had been trying to get a meeting with this gentleman since November. We finally coordinated a day and time for our informational meeting on how to start my entertainment-related business. Yay! The publicist is going to connect me with the COO of that business as well.

The day after I completed the experiment, a producer, who I had not heard from in years, called me out of the blue with an offer to serve as a producer on several of his projects. Also, he said he would give me producer credits even if I chose not to work on his projects.

These are some amazing results. I have continued to incorporate your Core 4 Formula into my morning and nighttime rituals. I even fall asleep to my audio Afformations.

Thank you, Noah!

SECTION III

YOUR BEST NEXT STEPS

- 13 -

THE CORE 4 AND YOU

*"The only questions that really matter
are the ones you ask yourself."*

— URSULA K. LE GUIN

Now that you know the four 'A's of my Afformations Method, and now that I've given you 301 of my favorite Millionaire Afformations, you may be wondering, "Noah, what should I do now that this book is almost over?"

Have no fear, Big Daddy Noah is here!

The first and most important thing you can do now is incorporate the practice of Afformations in your daily life. And the fastest and easiest way to do that is by using *my Core 4 Formula*.

Remember the Four Modes of Human Communication I taught you in chapter 3? Here's where you're going to put them into daily practice, using my Core 4 Formula.

CORE 4 PHASE 1: READING.

You're going to commit to spending one minute reading your new, empowering Afformations every morning. Starting immediately, every morning, you're going to pick up this book and read for one minute.

CORE 4 PHASE 2: WRITING.

After you've read this book (or one of my other books in this series) for one minute, next you're going to spend one minute writing your new, empowering Afformations following the process I taught you in chapter 3.

CORE 4 PHASE 3: SPEAKING.

After the Writing Phase, you're going to speak your new Afformations out loud for one minute. Yes, you're actually going to say your new Afformations out loud following the same process I taught you.

CORE 4 PHASE 4: LISTENING.

The final phase of my Core 4 Formula is to spend one minute listening to your new Afformations. To get started, get my free 60-Second Stress Buster iAfform® Audio at www.iAfform.com.

THE BENEFITS OF MY CORE 4 FORMULA

Whether you've had a specialized morning routine for a while or this is something new for you, there are many benefits of doing my Core 4 Formula. These benefits include:

- ✓ Reduced stress
- ✓ Increased creativity
- ✓ Getting in touch with your intuition
- ✓ Becoming a better communicator
- ✓ Releasing negative thoughts
- ✓ Accessing your inner wisdom

So how do you start doing this if you've never done anything like it before? Here are eleven additional tips to help you get started!

Tip #1: The process of doing my *Core 4 Formula* is as simple as it sounds. You're simply going to commit to yourself and the Universe that you're going to do all four phases of my Core 4 Formula every morning.

Why do we have to do them in the morning? Here are five reasons why:

Reason #1: When you're reading, writing, speaking, and listening in the morning, your brain is fresh and ready for new ideas.

Reason #2: Following this process in the morning is the best way to free your mind of negative thoughts before they have a chance to take root.

Reason #3: You will be able to act on your ideas much more effectively before the crush of daily events pushes your ideas out of your head.

MORNINGS ARE THE BEST TIME TO DO MY CORE 4 FORMULA.

Reason #4: Unlike the rest of the day, mornings are an easier time to think clearly and put your thoughts on the written page.

Reason #5: During this private time, you won't be interrupted, so you're free to read, write, speak, and listen to whatever you want.

Tip #2: Create a routine around this practice so you can avoid distractions that could make you feel rushed or overwhelmed. In fact, my Core 4 Formula is the best way I know to jumpstart your creative day.

Now you might be saying, "But Noah, I'm not creative!"

Of course, you're creative! You're human, aren't you? Human beings are, by our very nature, creative—and that includes you.

The process of creating doesn't mean that you have to share what you do with anyone else. Far from it—indeed, this time is for you and you alone. You never have to share your private thoughts with another person unless you choose to.

Tip #3: The process of reading, writing, speaking, and listening every day will enable you to tap into your inner wisdom, which will help you to find creative solutions to your problems. It's also a wonderful way to start the day because it allows you to express yourself and learn about what you want that you may have buried deep inside.

Tip #4: Adopting the Core 4 Formula is also an excellent way to get out of a rut and feel refreshed. For instance, if you're feeling stuck or unsure about anything in your life, it's one of the easiest ways to unblock, and it's an enjoyable practice to keep up with.

Tip #5: The Core 4 Formula is a fast and easy way to clear your mind. Whether you think you're creative or not, this time will allow you to focus on your creative side and release any stress you may be carrying.

It's a perfect way to relax, unwind, and start your day. The best thing to do is find the time to do these four simple things. You'll be surprised at how much you'll achieve by committing and doing this every day.

As you commit to doing your own Core 4 practice, you'll be surprised to see how it begins to change your life. You'll discover new insights and feel more alive!

Whether you think you're creative or not, following your Core 4 practice will quickly improve your overall well-being. You'll be amazed at how much you can accomplish.

USE THIS FORMULA TO QUICKLY CLEAR YOUR MIND OF CLUTTER.

Tip #6: It's important to have a consistent schedule and stick with it. As simple as it sounds, doing your Core 4 will become one of your favorite new daily habits—one you won't want to live without!

Tip #7: Remember that you're not doing this to impress anyone else. The intention is to read, write, speak, and listen so you clear your mind and access the abundance of the Universe.

No matter what you do, don't be discouraged; you'll be happier and more productive when you have a consistent Core 4 practice. And it will improve your mental health as well.

Tip #8: Keeping a **Millionaire Afformations Journal** can improve your life and help you get more done. Besides being one of the best ways to express yourself and your feelings, you'll also find that you can minimize your morning distractions.

Tip #9: In addition to boosting your confidence, you'll be able to express your fears, your plans, and your dreams. Regardless of your goals, you'll be able to achieve them a lot faster and easier when you follow my Core 4 Formula.

Tip #10: Begin this new daily practice starting immediately. Start first thing tomorrow because it's free, easy, and has many benefits. And did I mention—it's free?

Tip #11: Sounding perfect isn't the goal—doing it is! Remember, this is just for you, which means nobody needs to see it except you. For example, here's an actual excerpt from one of my Core 4 writing journals:

11:38 a.m. Well, it's still morning. I spent this morning vacuuming and cleaning, and blowing leaves. I have to get some noise-canceling earphones because my ears hurt after all that blowing. I have sensitive ears anyway.

Why am I enough?

Do you see what I did? I simply write about what's going on in my life at the time, then write Afformations to continue re-wiring my brain with even more empowering beliefs.

Yep, that's all there is to it.

Simple? Yes, incredibly simple.

Easy? Not necessarily.

I can hear the objections already:

"But Noah, I'm too busy . . ."

"But Noah, I have too much to do and too little time . . ."

"But Noah, I don't have a journal . . ."

Yeah, yeah, yeah.

> YOU CAN HAVE EXCUSES OR SUCCESS; PICK ONE.

All of these excuses are designed to keep you stuck right where you are. Bottom line: If you're happy with the results you're currently getting, then you shouldn't do anything differently.

If, however, you *do* want different results, the laws of the Universe require that you *do something different* in order to get those results.

"WHAT IF I WANT TO DO MORE?"

I've had many people say to me, "Noah, I love my Core 4 practice! Can I do *more* than four minutes a day?"

My answer: "Of course, you can!"

Here's my philosophy behind my Core 4 Formula. I created it to combat the single most popular excuse everyone uses for not changing their lives: "I'd love to change, but I just don't have the time."

My response to that excuse is, "You're telling me you don't have *four minutes a day* to change your life?"

If, for example, I told you that you had to meditate or do yoga or work on your chakras for an hour a day to change your life, you'd have a viable excuse for saying, "I don't have the time."

However, now that I've shown you that you can literally change your life in less than five minutes a day, I've taken away every excuse you could possibly have for *not* doing this.

Nevertheless, if you want to do more than one minute for each phase of my Core 4 Formula, by all means—go for it!

For instance, you could read this book for five minutes, write your new Afformations for ten minutes, say them out loud for a minute, and then listen to your iAfform® Audios for an hour while you're busy doing other things. (Remember, I designed iAfform Audios so you can listen to them and change your brain while you're not even paying attention!)

YOU CAN DO THIS PRACTICE FOR AS LONG AS YOU WANT, EACH DAY.

Here's another example. When I discovered Afformations in April 1997, I would write and write and write and write my Afformations in my journals for hours on end. I still have those journals, and they are filled with thousands of Afformations, representing hundreds of hours of me sitting there, writing them by hand.

It's up to you. You can do as many as you like for as long as you want and do your daily Core 4 practice as long as it makes sense for your individual situation.

The point is that my Core 4 Formula means that you have no more excuses for *not* doing this. Reading, writing, speaking, and listening to your new, empowering Afformations is the smartest, best, and most powerful way to start your day that's ever been discovered.

Heck, if you want to accelerate your results even faster, you can even *end* your day doing your Core 4 again before you go to bed! What better way to get a great night's sleep and ignite your inner creative power to manifest your desires than to reprogram your mind using my Afformations Method in the fastest, easiest, and most effective way possible?

And here's one bonus tip for you.

Tip #12: Get the *Millionaire Afformations Journal* to help you get even more benefit from the exercises in this book. In the Journal, I walk you through each step and show you even more ways to use my Core 4 Formula so you can get the most from your new Afformations practice every day.

Get yours now at www.MillionaireAfformations.com.

Now let's bring everything I've taught you in this book together so you can change your life using Afformations in the next fourteen days!

- 14 -

THE CHANGE YOUR LIFE WITH AFFORMATIONS® 14-DAY SPRINT

"Take the attitude of a student, never be too big to ask questions, never know too much to learn something new."

— OG MANDINO

Imagine that you are standing at the edge of a cliff. You're standing there overlooking a large canyon. On the other side of the canyon, you can see a pot of gold. What would you do? You'd likely do whatever it takes to get to the other side, right?

You wouldn't just stand there and think, *Wow, a pot of gold. Oh well, I'll never get there. I can't do it. Plus, I don't know how to get from here to there. I guess I'll just forget about it.*

No, you'd do *anything it takes* to get from where you are to where you want to be, right?

Here's an illustration to show you what I mean.

Let me explain this diagram further.

Right now, you are living in what I call your *Current Perceived Reality (CPR)*.

In your CPR, you do what you do, you have what you have, you know what you know, and you have the limitations you think you have. This is what you perceive your reality (your life) to be right now.

Where you want to get to (your Pot of Gold) is what I call your *New Desired Reality (NDR)*.

Your NDR is all the things you *want*—for example, more money, more influence, a new car, a new house, a better job, happier relationships, world peace, and so on.

The question is, what is standing between you (your CPR) and what you want (your NDR)?

Between your CPR and your NDR, there is a gap. And that gap is what I call *Your Belief Gap.*

For example, let's say you want to make more money in your business. Imagine if I were to ask you right now, "Do you think you can make more money in your business?"

You'd probably say, "Sure, Noah. I can do it!"

That's your *conscious* mind talking.

However, if we could hear what you were telling yourself in your *subconscious* mind, we might hear things like this. "I don't know if I can do it. I don't know how to do it. What if I'm not good enough? What if it doesn't work for me? Good people shouldn't want money, anyway. I should probably just forget about it."

If this is the case, what's happening for you right now looks like this.

In other words, you're in your CPR (Current Perceived Reality). You want to get to your NDR (New Desired Reality, also known as your Pot of Gold).

Yet between your CPR and your NDR lies Your Belief Gap—the subconscious belief that says, *I probably can't do it.*

BRIDGING THE GAP

In this book, I have given you the best, fastest, and most effective method ever discovered to change your beliefs and change your life: my Afformations Method.

When you look at it in this way, the purpose of using The Afformations Method is to bridge your Belief Gap—in other words, to change your beliefs from "I can't do it" to "What if I could do it?" to "Maybe I can do it" to "Of course, I can do it!"

Now that you've learned how to use my Afformations Method, you no longer need to use the old method—which, as you can now see, is attempting to force yourself to believe something you don't believe. Now, using my Afformations Method, you will simply employ your brain's embedded presupposition factor so that as you start asking empowering questions, your brain will automatically search for the answers.

And the result of those answers will become your new life.

So, the equation looks like this.

Better questions > Better answers > Better habits > Better results > A Better Life

THE THREE PILLARS OF TRANSFORMATION

Do a Google search on "how to change your life" or even "how to change your habits," and you'll find millions of articles and videos, and they all say something different. Some people say it takes thirty days to change a habit; some say longer, and some say shorter.

However, the reality is that you can change your life instantly when you have the right plan, the right tools, and the right support.

In our coaching, we call these *The Three Pillars of Transformation.* Here's what it looks like.

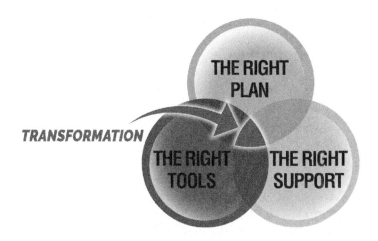

What happens when any one of these pillars is missing? Let me tell you a story to illustrate.

Earlier, I told you that when I was growing up, my father decided to build a house for our family to live in. The first thing he did was create a blueprint. That meant he had a good plan.

Then he assembled his tools—hammer, saw, nails, cement, wood, etc. So, he had the right tools.

However, because he never got the final pillar—the right support—my dad was always scrambling to finish the house; indeed, our house was never finished.

In addition, because he never got the right support, the bank foreclosed on us, and we were forced to move out of that house when I was fifteen years old.

The moral of the story is that even if you have two out of three Pillars of Transformation, it's going to be very, very difficult for you to go from where you are (your CPR) to where you want to be (your NDR, or Pot of Gold).

HERE'S WHAT THIS MEANS FOR YOU

In this book, I've given you **the right plan**—my Afformations Method. Using Afformations, you can literally change any negative belief into a positive belief instantly. Yes, in less than ten seconds!

I've also given you **the right tools**—for example, I've given you The Four A's of The Afformations Method, I've taught you The Four Modes of Human Communication, I've given you my Core 4 Formula, and I've also shown you where you can get done-for-you iAfform Audio recordings at **www.iAfform.com** so you can change your beliefs while you're not even paying attention.

So, what's next?

What's next is for you to *get the right support* so you can make these changes stick—so you can finally go from your CPR to your NDR and reach the Pot of Gold at the end of the rainbow.

What does the right support look like?

Whether you choose to do it on your own or whether you choose to do it with me and my team at **www.SuccessClinic.com** so you can accelerate your results even faster, these are the four steps you need to do, now that this book is almost over.

STEP 1: ASK YOURSELF WHAT YOU REALLY WANT.

This is the first A of my Afformations Method that I taught you in chapter 3. The irony is that of the thousands of people I've coached over the last quarter-century, many of them came to me not even knowing what they wanted. This means if you don't know what you want, you're going to have an awfully hard time getting there.

Like my grocery store examples from earlier in this book, if you don't know where you're going or don't know why you're going there, you'll just be driving around in circles.

That's why this is the most important and foundational step to going from your CPR to your Pot of Gold.

STEP 2: AFFORM THAT WHAT YOU REALLY WANT IS ALREADY TRUE.

As I showed you in chapter 3, Afformations employ the embedded presupposition factor of the brain, which means that your brain is hard-wired to search for answers to questions.

Most people are unconsciously asking disempowering questions like, "Why am I so stupid?" and "Why am I so broke?"

These questions are, in fact, creating their lives.

That's one reason why using Afformations is so incredibly powerful and transformational—because rather than trying to convince yourself of something you don't believe, you'll be using your brain's Automatic Search Function to make your new empowering questions a reality.

STEP 3: ACCEPT THE TRUTH OF YOUR NEW QUESTIONS.

Use my Core 4 Formula I taught you in the previous chapter. Read your new Afformations, write them in your Millionaire Afformations Journal, say them out loud to your friends and family (or while you're alone), and listen to the done-for-you iAfform® Audios every day for at least one minute each (and, of course, you can go longer if you so desire).

The more you do my Core 4 Formula, the faster you will change your subconscious thought patterns from *I can't do it* to *Of course I can do it!*

STEP 4: ACT BASED ON YOUR NEW ASSUMPTIONS.

Afformations are not magic; they're science. *You're already using Afformations anyway!* Now that you've been exposed to my teaching methods, you can begin to turn what has been unconscious and disempowering into a process that is conscious and empowering.

Will it take you fourteen days to change your life?

In fact, countless people over the last twenty-five years have told me that using my Afformations Method changed their lives in an instant. Many have told me that the moment they started using Afformations, they felt an immediate sense of calm, peace, and happiness wash over them—something they hadn't felt in years . . . or ever!

YOU CAN CHANGE YOUR LIFE IN AN INSTANT USING MY AFFORMATIONS METHOD.

Naturally, some Afformations take longer to manifest than others. For instance, you can't simply Afform, "Why do I have a million dollars in the bank?" and expect a million dollars to magically appear in your bank account overnight. (That would be nice, though, wouldn't it?) The Universe just doesn't work that way.

As I've stated, Afformations are the foundation of everything we do at SuccessClinic.com, and you should make them the foundation of your daily habits and routine.

And if you'd like some help doing that . . .

HERE'S HOW I CAN HELP YOU

Because of the outpouring of love from Afformers like you from around the globe who have seen their lives change because of using my Afformations Method, I've created many ways for you to get the right support you need to achieve the results you desire in your life, health, career, and relationships.

Step One: Subscribe to my YouTube channel at **www.WatchNoahTV.com** to discover my latest insights and best practices on Inner Game and Outer Game Mastery and how to live a 7-Figure Life.

Step Two: Join my legendary **AFFORMATIONS**® **Advantage Online Learning Academy**, so you can get my help to make Afformations part of your daily habits and daily routine.

By the end of this 14-day journey, you'll have the tools you need to change negative beliefs into positive *action* so you can create a truly happy, fulfilling, and rich life.

You'll get:

#1: The Complete AFFORMATIONS® Blueprint

I will give you my entire detailed system of how I consistently help people instantly change their beliefs and rapidly change their lives.

#2: The "I Don't Think This Will Work for Me" Method

How to convert negative beliefs into unstoppable self-confidence in just five minutes a day.

#3: The Need for Speed Clinic

How to master the skill set that truly separates the top 0.1%.

#4: Laser Coaching and Q&A

You'll get recordings of my client coaching calls, so you can discover how to crush your negative self-talk.

You'll also get guided AFFORMATIONS from me, The Father of AFFORMATIONS®, along with thousands of dollars in added bonuses. Get *The AFFORMATIONS® Advantage* now at **www.Afformations.com**.

Step Three: Call, text, or email one or more people today, and invite them to join you for The Millionaire Afformations 14-Day Sprint. Send them to **www.MillionaireAfformations.com** so they can embark on this journey with you, so the two (or more) of you can support, encourage, and hold each other accountable.

Be sure to get a copy of ***Millionaire AFFORMATIONS® Journal*** (the companion journal to this book), so you can make my Core 4 Formula part of your everyday routine. Yes, it's true: you can change your mental, emotional and financial life while you're making your morning coffee!

Get your copy of the *Millionaire AFFORMATIONS® Journal* now at **www.MillionaireAfformations.com/journal**

IMPORTANT: Don't wait until you have an accountability partner on board to start using Afformations and my Core 4 Formula. In fact, you can start using the exercises in this book and *Millionaire AFFORMATIONS® Journal* right now.

Because whether or not you've found someone to come on this journey with you, I still recommend starting to use Afformations immediately.

That's one of the beautiful aspects of using my Afformations Method—you take your brain with you everywhere you go!

That means, *starting right now*, you can begin to change any disempowering thought or belief into an empowering Afformation, anytime, anywhere, day or night.

Then, you'll be even more capable of inspiring others to start using Afformations after you've already experienced a few days of doing it. So, start now!

Then, as soon as you can, invite a friend, family member, team member, or colleague to join you. You can even share your experience with this book as well as the *Millionaire AFFORMATIONS® Journal* and the Core 4 Formula.

ARE YOU READY TO TAKE YOUR LIFE TO THE NEXT LEVEL?

What is the next level in your personal or professional life? Which areas need to be transformed to reach that level? Give yourself the gift of investing just five minutes a day to make significant improvements in your life, one day at a time. No matter what your past has been, you *can* change your future by simply changing the questions you're asking yourself, starting *right now!*

CONCLUSION

"Einstein was a man who could ask immensely simple questions. And what his life showed, and his work, is that when the answers are simple too, then you hear God thinking."

— JACOB BRONOWSKI

It was a dark and stormy night.

Aboard the mighty battleship *Missouri*, the captain and first officer stood on the bridge, looking out into the stormy seas. Suddenly, a light appeared in the distance through the thick fog. A ship was right in their path!

The captain said to the first officer, "Signal them to move to starboard."

"Aye-aye, Captain." Over the signal lamp, the signalman sent the message using Morse code, *Starboard.*

A few moments later, the signal came back, *Starboard yourself.*

"What!" the captain shouted. "Tell them who we are and tell them to move to starboard immediately!"

The signalman sent the message: *This is the mighty Missouri. Starboard!*

A few moments later, the signal came back: *This is the lighthouse. Your call.*

The principles and tools I've taught you in this book are like the lighthouse; they don't move. We can crash ourselves against them, or we can use them to guide our forward progress.

Now that this book is over, you can choose to go back to your old way of thinking; but why would you?

As I've stated repeatedly, you and I and every other human being are already using my Afformations Method every moment of our lives.

However, *you* now have the ultimate advantage, because now you know exactly how to change your beliefs at the subconscious level, which means *starting right now*, you can change the trajectory of your life.

START USING AFFORMATIONS NOW, BECAUSE IT WILL CHANGE YOUR LIFE FOR THE BETTER.

Starting today, the choices you make and the actions you take will determine who you will be and where you'll end up for the rest of your life. Therefore, don't put off creating and experiencing the happiness, health, wealth, success, and love that you desire.

If you want your life to improve, you must improve yourself first. With or without an accountability partner, commit to using Afformations immediately so you can begin accessing more of your potential than you ever imagined possible.

Imagine . . . just fourteen days from now, you will be well on your way to transforming every area of your life!

LET'S KEEP HELPING OTHERS

May I ask you a quick favor?

If this book has added value to your life, if you feel like you're better off after reading it, and if you see that Afformations can help you take any (or every) area of your life to the next level, I'm hoping you'll do something for someone you care about.

Give this book to them. Let them borrow your copy. Ask them to read it so they have the opportunity to transform their life for the better.

Or, if you're not willing to give up your copy quite yet because you're planning on going back and re-reading it, you can get them their own copy.

It could be for no special occasion at all other than to say, "Hey, I love and appreciate you, and I want to help you live your best life. Read this."

If you believe, as I do, that being a great friend, family member, or colleague is about helping your friends and loved ones to become the best versions of themselves, I encourage you to share this book with them.

Together, we are truly *elevating the consciousness of Earth, one question at a time.*

Thank you so much!

FOR THOSE
WHO WANT TO GO
FURTHER AND FASTER

"If breaking a habit has been hard for you to do,
then a helping hand is in order."

— KENNETH SCHWARZ

When I discovered Afformations in April 1997, I knew that I had found something that would revolutionize the personal growth industry. Because The Afformations Method is so simple, yet so profound and transformational, I had a vision that millions of people around the world would one day be using my method.

The irony is, even though my vision was crystal clear in my mind, I didn't know how to achieve it. So, I kept searching and searching for how to make my vision a reality.

Then, on October 20, 1997, I made a second discovery that changed my life. I discovered the hidden condition that causes millions of people to hold themselves back from the success they're capable of. I called that condition *success anorexia* because millions of people are unknowingly and unconsciously *starving themselves of success.*

It was only after my second epiphany that I knew what I had to do—begin writing, coaching, and speaking about Afformations and success anorexia.

So that's what I did.

First came *Permission to Succeed*˚.

Then *The Secret Code of Success*.

Then *The Book of Afformations*˚.

Then *Power Habits*˚.

And now, the book you're holding in your hands (or listening to).

As a result, I became the only author in the history of publishing to have works published by Hay House, HarperCollins, Simon & Schuster, Mindvalley, Nightingale-Conant, and the *Chicken Soup for the Soul* publisher.

Through all of this, one fact became abundantly clear—as miraculous as Afformations are to change your life, we still need more. That's because we humans are complex creatures and because success itself is so varied and multi-layered.

I realized that to fulfill my mission of *elevating the consciousness of Earth, one question at a time*, I had to create a complete, all-encompassing system that would cover all areas of life, work, and how to achieve fulfillment, success, and self-mastery.

AFFORMATIONS ARE THE FOUNDATIONAL STEP OF THE POWER HABITS® SYSTEM.

That's why I created *The Power Habits® System*.

The Power Habits System is the culmination of my twenty-five years of coaching high achievers toward even greater success, happiness, and fulfillment in their lives and work.

Let me give you an analogy to illustrate the point.

Let's say you decide one day that you want to buy a new house. You get into your car and start driving around the neighborhood you want to live in. Do you drive around and say, "Wow, look at all those nice foundations?"

No, you're looking at all the beautiful houses! In fact, you don't even notice the foundations.

However, without a strong foundation, is your new house going to be solid? Nope, it's going to collapse because the foundation is the beginning of building a strong, solid house.

It's the same with Afformations and Power Habits. Afformations are the foundation of The Power Habits System because Afformations are the fastest, easiest way to change your beliefs that's ever been invented.

As powerful and life-changing as Afformations are, they are not the entire house. That's why we need the rest of The Power Habits System to create the health, wealth, happiness, and fulfillment that we truly desire.

Here is an illustration of The Power Habits System to show you what it looks like.

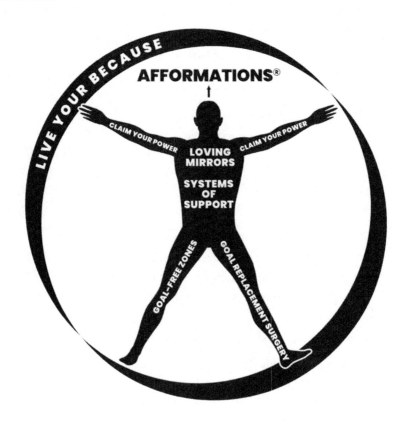

As you can see, Afformations are the starting point, which means you now have everything you need to build the foundation of your new house—I mean, your new life.

Now, if you'd like to go further even faster, I recommend the following steps:

Step 1: Subscribe to my YouTube channel at **www.WatchNoahTV.com**, because you'll discover my latest insights and best practices on Afformations, Power Habits, Inner Game and Outer Game Mastery, and a variety of other subjects to help you live a 7-Figure Life.

Step 2: Join Power Habits® Academy at **www.PowerHabitsAcademy.com**.

Because by the end of this coaching intensive, you'll discover how to use my legendary Power Habits® System to admit what you truly desire, identify exactly what's stopping you from having it, and give yourself permission to live a joyfully happy, fulfilling and rich life.

Step 3: If you'd like to accelerate your results even faster, watch my free video training at **www.FreeGiftfromNoah.com**.

There, you'll discover how I help my clients make more in just twelve weeks than they made in the previous twelve months, while gaining one to three hours in their day and four to eight weeks per year.

"Noah St. John's coaching starts where Think and Grow Rich *and* The Secret *left off!"*

— Mike Filsaime, Eight-Figure CEO of Groove.cm

"My company went from being stuck at $4M in sales to over $20M in sales as a result of coaching with Noah!"

— Adam S., Eight-Figure CEO

"My income is up 800% since I started coaching with Noah!"

— Steven B., Entrepreneur

RECOMMENDED RESOURCES

YOUR FREE BONUS GIFT

As a thank-you for purchasing this book, I would like to give you a free *60-Second Stress Buster iAfform® Audio.*

iAfform® Audios are done-for-you, downloadable audio recordings of 101 of my favorite empowering AFFORMATIONS set to inspiring music.

They will help you change your subconscious thought patterns while you're busy doing other things, which means you can begin to attract more abundance without the struggle.

As I've mentioned earlier, you can listen to your iAfform Audios anytime, anywhere—while you're eating or exercising, working, or playing, in the car, on your laptop, or in your office. You can even listen to your iAfform Audios while you sleep!

I've created iAfform Audios to help you accelerate your results in the most important areas of life, including:

- *Ultimate Wealth*
- *Ultimate Business Success*
- *Ultimate Self-Confidence*
- *Ultimate Love*
- *Deep, Blissful Sleep*
- *No More Stress*
- *Live Your Life Purpose*
- . . . and many more

"Noah, I just signed my first million-dollar deal from a single client. It would not have been possible without applying what you taught me about creating a wealthy mindset."

— Robert S., Entrepreneur

"Hi, Noah. I got the iAfform Audios on Stress, Love, Confidence, Sleep, Business, Wealth, and Soul Mission. I have now slept without sedation for two weeks. I have fibromyalgia, and insomnia is one of the symptoms. It is a whole new life for me to sleep without aids; I feel less tired during the day and more focused. I am also now starting to feel confident enough to speak publicly to promote my healing practice. Thank you so very much!"

— Claudette C., Ontario, Canada

Claim your free 60-Second iAfform Audio Stress Buster at

iAfform.com

BOOK NOAH TO SPEAK

*"Noah is definitely NOT your typical motivational speaker!
I took six pages of notes during his keynote presentation.
SIMPLY PHENOMENAL—A MUST-HAVE RESOURCE
for every organization that wants to grow!"*

— Mary Kay Cosmetics

*"All I heard was great feedback!
Thank you, Noah, for really engaging our audience.
I am recommending you as a speaker for more meetings."*

— Meeting Planners International

*"I highly recommend Noah St. John as a keynote speaker because
he resonates on a deep emotional level with his audience.
Dynamic, impactful, inspiring, motivating, and professional—
in short, the PERFECT speaker!"*

— City Summit & Gala

Book Noah as your keynote speaker, and you're guaranteed to make your event highly enjoyable and unforgettable.

For more than two decades, Noah St. John has consistently rated as the #1 keynote speaker by meeting planners and attendees.

His unique style combines inspiring audiences with his remarkable TRUE story, keeping them laughing with his high-energy, down-to-earth style, and empowering them with actionable strategies to take their RESULTS to the NEXT LEVEL.

Book Noah for your event at
BookNoah.com

ALSO AVAILABLE FROM NOAH ST. JOHN

THE 12-WEEK BREAKTHROUGH

How I Help My Clients Make More in Just 12 Weeks
Than They Made in the Past 12 Months—
While Gaining 1–3 Hours per Day and 4–8 Weeks a Year.

12WeekBreakthrough.com

POWER HABITS® ACADEMY

Take Out Your Head Trash About Money,
Admit What You Truly Desire
and Experience Your Quantum Leap.

PowerHabitsAcademy.com

THE AFFORMATIONS® ADVANTAGE

Immediately Attract More Abundance on Autopilot.

Afformations.com

Shop our complete line of business and personal growth programs:

ShopNoahStJohn.com

Book Noah to speak at your virtual or live event:

BookNoah.com

MOTIVATE AND INSPIRE OTHERS!

"SHARE THIS BOOK"

RETAIL $24.95

Special Quantity Discounts Available

To Place an Order, Contact:

(330) 871-4331

info@SuccessClinic.com

NOAHSTJOHN.COM

NOAH ST. JOHN
#1 BESTSELLING
AUTHOR OF

THE BOOK OF AFFORMATIONS®

CREATOR OF
THE 12-WEEK BREAKTHROUGH

Special FREE Bonus Gift for You

**Experience This FREE Masterclass with Dr. Noah St. John,
"The Mental Health Coach to the Stars"**

"How I Help My Clients Make More in Just 12 Weeks
Than They Did in the Past 12 Months,
While Gaining 1–3 Hours per Day and 4–8 Weeks a Year."

You Will Discover . . .

SECRET #1: The Forgotten Wealth Secret
SECRET #2: The "RAP Factor" Method for Riches
SECRET #3: The "ATM Formula" for Automatic Success

Accelerate your success by claiming your ***FREE*** *Bonus Gift:*

FreeGiftFromNoah.com

ACKNOWLEDGMENTS

My Most Grateful Thanks to . . .

God, the answer to all of our questions.

My beautiful wife, Babette, for being my best friend and the best Loving Mirror I've ever had. Thank you for believing in me and supporting me and for your tireless commitment to helping me put a dent in the universe.

My parents, who sacrificed and gave more than they had.

Jack Canfield, for grokking my message when it was a bunch of pages bound with a piece of tape.

Dr. Stephen R. Covey, who inspired me to get into the business of helping people when the cassette album of The 7 Habits of Highly Effective People fell off a church bookshelf and landed at my feet. I swear I'm not making that up.

Through the years, many have shared ideas, inspiration, mentoring, and support that have impacted my life, each in a different way. While it's impossible to thank everyone, please know that I appreciate you greatly:

Alex Mandossian, Arianna Huffington, Barbara De Angelis, Donny Osmond, Gary Vaynerchuk, Jenny McCarthy, Joel Osteen, John Lee Dumas, Marie Forleo, Marie Osmond, Suze Orman, Adam Farfan, Anik Singal, Ashley Massengill, Dr. Brad Nelson, Brian Kurtz, Chris Stoikos, Dan Bova, Daniel Marcos, David Meltzer, David Deutsch, David Hancock, Dr. Fabrizio Mancini, Glenn Morshower, Harvey Mackay, Jason Hewlett, Jay Abraham, Jeff Magee, Jeffrey Hayzlett, Jen Groover, JJ Virgin, Jim Kwik, Joe Polish, Joe Vitale, John Assaraf, John Cito, Dr. John Gray,

Jon Benson, Kat Parker-Merritt, Dr. Kellyann Petrucci, Kody Bateman, Lisa Nichols, Lisa Sasevich, Mari Smith, MaryEllen Tribby, Mike Filsaime, Nathan Osmond, Neale Donald Walsch, Noah Kagan, Peng Joon, Peter Hoppenfeld, Ray Higdon, Reid Tracy, Rich Schefren, Richard Rossi, Russell Brunson, Tom Junod, Walter O'Brien, Verne Harnish, Yanik Silver, and so many other people who have helped me in my career!

To Oprah, thank you in advance for our Super Soul Sunday interview - *Why was it your most-watched inspirational show ever?* And, of course, for all of the inspiration you've provided in my life.

I'm extremely grateful to my new marketing, editorial, and design team, who contributed their special talents to this book. Extra special thanks to Honorée Corder, who contributed so much to the creation and marketing of this book; Terry Stafford, editor extraordinaire; and Dino Marino for your unparalleled design skills.

Very special thanks to the vast and growing tribe of our phenomenal coaching clients around the world who believe in the power of this message. Thank you for spreading the word about my work to all corners of the globe!

Every day, as I hear more and more stories of how the coaching work we do together is changing lives, you inspire, encourage, and uplift me.

I am humbled by your stories of how my work has changed your lives—truly, more than you know. Whether you're a member of our Coaching Family, attend one of our virtual events or online trainings this year, or simply commit to telling your friends about this book, I'm grateful for you.

Every day brings with it the opportunity to be reborn in the next greatest version of ourselves.

NOW IT'S YOUR TURN— I LOOK FORWARD TO BEING A PART OF YOUR SUCCESS STORY!

ABOUT THE AUTHOR

NOAH ST. JOHN, PhD is recognized as "The Father of AFFORMATIONS®" and "The Mental Health Coach to the Stars."

Working with Hollywood celebrities, eight-figure company CEOs, professional athletes, top executives, and elite entrepreneurs, Noah is famous for helping his coaching clients make more in twelve weeks than they did in the previous twelve months while gaining 1–3 hours per day and 4–8 weeks a year.

Noah's clients are the 0.1% rock stars who love to *take action* and get amazing *results*.

Noah is also the only author in history to have works published by HarperCollins, Hay House, Simon & Schuster, Mindvalley, Nightingale-Conant, and the *Chicken Soup for the Soul* publisher. His seventeen books have been published in eighteen languages worldwide.

Noah's mission is to eliminate not-enoughness from the world, and he is internationally known for his signature coaching services and facilitating workshops at companies and institutions across the globe. Noah delivers private workshops, virtual events, and online courses that his audiences call "MANDATORY for anyone who wants to succeed in life and business."

One of the most requested, in-demand business and motivational keynote speakers in the world, Noah is famous for having "The Midas Touch" because his coaching clients have added more than $2.7 billion in sales. His sought-after advice is known as the "secret sauce" to business and personal growth.

He also appears frequently in the news worldwide, including ABC, NBC, CBS, FOX, The Hallmark Channel, National Public Radio, *Chicago Sun-Times*, *Parade*, *Los Angeles Business Journal*, *The Washington Post*, *Woman's Day*, *Entrepreneurs on Fire*, *Selling Power*, Entrepreneur.com, *The Jenny McCarthy Show*, *Costco Connection*, and *SUCCESS* magazine.

Fun fact: Noah once won an all-expenses-paid trip to Hawaii on the game show *Concentration*, where he missed winning a new car by three seconds. (Note: He had not yet discovered his Afformations® Method or Power Habits® Formula.)

Book Noah to speak for your event at **www.BookNoah.com**.

HONORÉE CORDER is an author and book strategist with more than fifty published books and four million sold worldwide in thirty-nine languages. You can find out more at HonoreeCorder.com.

Printed in Great Britain
by Amazon

42669987R00086